THE
CHRISTMAS
BOOK OF LISTS

The CHRISTMAS Book of Lists

Fun-to-Read Lists & Facts
about the
World's Favorite Holiday

by Elizabeth Haynie

Kingsley Press
Downers Grove, Illinois

Copyright 1994 by Anton Enterprises, Inc.
All rights reserved.

No part of this book may be reproduced, or transmitted in any form or by any means, electronic or mechanical, including photocopying, recording or by any information storage and retrieval system without written permission from the publisher.

Published by Kingsley Press
P.O. Box 606, Downers Grove, IL 60516

Published in the United States of America

ISBN 0-9637195-0-5

TABLE OF CONTENTS

1. It Happened on Christmas   7
including . . . 20 People Born on Christmas Day, What 3 Popes Were Doing on Christmas Day, 32 Songs That Were #1 on the Billboard Charts on Christmas Day . . . and more

2. The Sounds of Christmas   22
including . . . 15 Holiday Songs with the Word "Christmas" in the Title, 7 Christmas Songs Introduced by Bing Crosby, 6 "Christmas" Songs That Don't Mention Christmas . . . and more

3. From Page to Screen to Stage   39
including . . . 6 Reasons George Bailey Never Leaves Bedford Falls, 4 Stars Known for Their Christmas Television Specials, 9 Filmed Versions of A Christmas Carol . . . and more

4. Christmas around the World   65
including . . . 7 Popular Holiday Beverages . . . Where the Gifts Are Left in 8 Countries . . . How Children in 6 Countries Circulate Their Christmas Lists . . . and more

5. A Holiday Potpourri   74
including . . . 7 States with Cities Called Bethlehem, 9 Toys That Never Go Out of Style, 10 Items You See at the Grocery Store More Often at Christmas . . . and more

Photo album of Christmas celebrations follows page 38.

Chapter 1
It Happened on Christmas

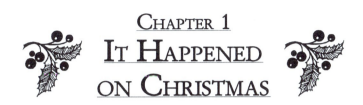

20 PEOPLE BORN ON CHRISTMAS DAY

1. Clara Barton, U.S. founder of the Red Cross, 1818
2. Humphrey Bogart, U.S. actor, 1899
3. Jimmy Buffett, U.S. singer and beach lover, 1946
4. Cab Calloway, U.S. bandleader, 1908
5. Louis Chevrolet, U.S. car manufacturer, 1878
6. Alice Cooper (born Vincent Furnier), U.S. rock star, 1948
7. Larry Csonka, U.S. football player, 1946
8. Conrad Hilton, U.S. hotelier, 1887
9. Barbara Mandrell, U.S. singer, 1948
10. Tony Martin, U.S. singer, 1914
11. Sir Isaac Newton, British physicist, 1642
12. Little Richard (born Richard Penniman), U.S. rock legend, 1935
13. Robert L. Ripley, U.S. cartoonist and chronicler of the unusual, 1893
14. Anwar Sadat, Egyptian president, 1918
15. Alexander Scriabin, Russian composer, 1872
16. Rod Serling, U.S. television producer, 1924
17. Sissy Spacek, U.S. actress, 1950
18. Ken Stabler, U.S. football player, 1946
19. Dorothy Wordsworth, British diarist and sister of William, 1771
20. Dame Rebecca West, British journalist and novelist, 1892

8 PEOPLE WHO DIED ON CHRISTMAS DAY

1. Johnny Ace, U.S. singer, 1954
2. Joan Blondell, movie actress, 1979
3. Samuel de Champlain, explorer, 1635
4. Charlie Chaplin, silent screen legend, 1977
5. W. C. Fields, movie actor, 1946
6. "Billy" Martin, baseball manager, 1989
7. Joan Miro, Spanish artist, 1983
8. Nick the Greek, U.S. gambler, 1966

6 MILITARY EVENTS THAT TOOK PLACE ON THE CHRISTMAS HOLIDAY

1. The Continental Army defeats Hessian soliders stationed at Trenton, New Jersey on Christmas Day 1776. Led by General George Washington, the Continental Army's task was made easier because the Hessians were participating in a little Christmas revelry.

2. The Treaty of Ghent is signed on Christmas Eve 1814, officially ending the War of 1812.

3. Warring British and German soldiers put down their guns for a few minutes to sing Christmas carols together on the Western Front, Christmas Day 1915.

4. Hong Kong surrenders to Japan, Christmas Day 1941.

5. General Dwight D. Eisenhower is named Supreme Commander of the European Forces, Christmas Eve 1943.

6. The Battle of the Bulge takes place at Bastogne, France, Christmas Day 1946.

IT HAPPENED ON CHRISTMAS

5 ROMANTIC EVENTS THAT TOOK PLACE DURING THE HOLIDAY SEASON

1. George Washington marries Martha Custis, Twelfth Night 1759.
2. Thomas Jefferson marries Martha Skelton, New Year's Day 1772.
3. James Polk marries Sarah Childress, New Year's Day 1824.
4. Luci Baines Johnson is engaged to Patrick Nugent, Christmas Eve 1965.
5. Gregory Peck marries Veronique Passani on New Year's Eve 1955.

10 THINGS EBENEZER SCROOGE DID ON CHRISTMAS DAY

According to his creator, Charles Dickens, Ebenezer Scrooge was a pretty busy guy on Christmas morning. Most movie versions of A Christmas Carol *don't have time to show everything the reformed miser did. Here's how he filled the day.*

1. Sends a prize turkey to his clerk, Bob Cratchit.

2. Shaves (while shaking with happiness and dancing).

3. Gets dressed "all in his best."

4. Approaches two men he had rudely turned away from his office the day before and tells them he *would* like to contribute to their charity. (The amount must have been very large, for Dickens has Scrooge whisper it into one of the gentleman's ear.)

5. Goes to church.

6. Goes for a long walk.

7. Watches the people hurrying to and fro.

8. Pats children on the head.

9. Questions beggars.

10. Visits his nephew, Fred (where they have a "wonderful party, wonderful games, wonderful unanimity, won-der-ful [sic] happiness!").

32 SONGS THAT WERE #1 ON THE BILLBOARD CHARTS ON CHRISTMAS DAY

1. "Dominque" by Sister Luc-Gabrielle, 1963
2. "Come See about Me" by the Supremes, 1964
3. "Over and Over" by the Dave Clark Five, 1965
4. "Good Vibrations" by the Beach Boys, 1966
5. "Daydream Believer" by The Monkees, 1967
6. "I Heard It through the Grapevine" by Marvin Gaye, 1968
7. "Leaving on a Jet Plane" by Peter, Paul, and Mary, 1969
8. "The Tears of a Clown" by Smokey Robinson and the Miracles, 1970
9. "Brand New Key" by Melanie, 1971
10. "Me and Mrs. Jones" by Billy Paul, 1972
11. "The Most Beautiful Girl" by Charlie Rich, 1973
12. "Cat's in the Cradle" by Harry Chapin, 1974
13. "Fly Robin Fly" by Silver Convention, 1975
14. "Tonight's the Night" by Rod Stewart, 1976
15. "How Deep Is Your Love?" by the Bee Gees, 1977
16. "Le Freak" by Chic, 1978
17. "Escape (The Piña Colada Song)" by Rupert Holmes, 1979
18. "Lady" by Kenny Rogers, 1980
19. "Physical" by Olivia Newton-John, 1981
20. "Maneater" by Hall and Oates, 1982
21. "Say, Say, Say" by Paul McCartney and Michael Jackson, 1983
22. "Like a Virgin" by Madonna, 1984
23. "Say You, Say Me" by Lionel Ritchie, 1985
24. "Walk Like an Egyptian" by The Bangles, 1986
25. "Faith" by George Michael, 1987
26. "Waiting for a Star to Fall" by Boy Meets Girl, 1988
27. "Another Day in Paradise" by Phil Collins, 1989
28. "Because I Love You" by Stevie B., 1990
29. "Black and White" by Michael Jackson, 1991
30. "I Will Always Love You" by Whitney Houston, 1992
31. "Hero" by Mariah Carey, 1993
32. "Here Comes the Hotstepper" by Ini Kamoze, 1994

5 BUSINESSES THAT GENERALLY REMAIN OPEN ON CHRISTMAS DAY

1. Hospitals
2. Gas stations
3. Large grocery store chains
4. Convenience stores
5. Professional and college sports

2 THINGS GEORGE WASHINGTON DID ON THE CHRISTMAS HOLIDAY

1. Crossed the Delaware River on Christmas Day 1776 with his Continental Army troops to stage a surprise attack on Hessian troops stationed in Trenton, New Jersey. This victory was a turning point in the Revolutionary War.

2. Resigned his commission as commander of the Continental Army on Christmas Eve 1783.

2 BARNYARD MIRACLES THAT "OCCUR" EVERY CHRISTMAS AT MIDNIGHT

1. Oxen kneel.
2. Cattle talk.

9 EVENTS THAT OCCURRED DURING MEDIEVAL CHRISTMASES

1. Clovis I, King of the Franks, is baptized a Christian, 503 A.D.
2. The legendary King Arthur removes the sword from the stone.
3. Charlemagne is crowned emperor by Pope Leo III, 800 A.D.
4. William the Conquerer assumes the English throne, 1066 A.D.
5. The English barons give King John their list of demands, 1214.
6. Baldwin I is crowned King of Jerus, 1100.
7. Roger II is crowned King of Sicily, 1130.
8. Henry VI, Holy Roman Emperor, is crowned King of Sicily, 1194.
9. Frederick II is elected King of Germany, 1196.

WHAT 3 POPES WERE DOING ON CHRISTMAS DAY

1. POPE GREGORY VII

   Kidnapped while saying Christmas Mass, 1075 A.D.

2. POPE LEO III

   Crowned Charlemagne Holy Roman Emperor, 800 A.D.

3. POPE JOHN XXIII

   Issued a papal bull convening the Roman Catholic Church's Twenty-First Ecumenical Council to be held in 1962.

10 MOVIES REVIEWED IN THE *NEW YORK TIMES* ON CHRISTMAS DAY

1. *The Prince of Tides*, December 25, 1991
2. *Alice*, December 25, 1990
3. *The Godfather, Part III*, December 25, 1990
4. *Green Card*, December 25, 1990
5. *Music Box*, December 25, 1989
6. *Brighton Beach Memoirs*, December 25, 1986

7. *The Morning After*, December 25, 1986
8. *Revolution*, December 25, 1985
9. *Altered States*, December 25, 1980
10. *Going in Style*, December 25, 1979

7 MUSICAL SOUNDTRACKS OR ORIGINAL CAST RECORDINGS THAT WERE IN *BILLBOARD'S* TOP 10 ON CHRISTMAS DAY

1. *West Side Story* (soundtrack), 1962
2. *South Pacific* (soundtrack), 1958
3. *The Sound of Music* (original cast), 1960
4. *My Fair Lady* (original cast), 1956
5. *The Music Man* (original cast), 1958
6. *Around the World in 80 Days* (soundtrack), 1957
7. *Gigi* (soundtrack), 1958

22 NOVELS THAT WERE #1 NEW YORK TIMES BESTSELLERS ON CHRISTMAS DAY

1. *Burr* by Gore Vidal, 1973
2. *Centennial* by James M. Michener, 1974
3. *Curtain* by Agatha Christie, 1975
4. *Sleeping Murder* by Agatha Christie, 1976
5. *The Silmarillion* by J. R. R. Tolkien, 1977
6. *Chesapeake* by James M. Michener, 1978
7. *The Establishment* by Howard Fast, 1979
8. *The Covenant* by James M. Michener, 1980
9. *An Indecent Obsession* by Colleen McCullough, 1981
10. *Space* by James M. Michener, 1982
11. *Pet Sematary* by Stephen King, 1983
12. *The Talisman* by Stephen King and Peter Straub, 1984
13. *The Mammoth Hunters* by Jean M. Auel, 1985
14. *The Mammoth Hunters* by Jean M. Auel, 1986
15. *Windmills of the Gods* by Sidney Sheldon, 1987
16. *The Sands of Time* by Sidney Sheldon, 1988
17. *The Dark Half* by Stephen King, 1989

18. *The Bad Place* by Dean R. Koontz, 1990
19. *Scarlett* by Alexandra Ripley, 1991
20. *Angel* by Johanna Lindsey, 1992
21. *Slow Waltz in Cedar Bend* by Robert James Waller, 1993
22. *Disclosure* by Michael Crichton, 1994

22 NON-FICTION BOOKS THAT WERE #1 *NEW YORK TIMES* BEST-SELLERS ON CHRISTMAS DAY

1. *Alistair Cooke's America* by Alistair Cook, 1973
2. *All Things Bright and Beautiful* by James Herriott, 1974
3. *The Relaxation Response* by Herbert Benson, M.D., 1975
4. *Roots* by Alex Haley, 1976
5. *All Things Wise and Wonderful* by James Herriott, 1977
6. *Mommie Dearest* by Christina Crawford, 1978
7. *Aunt Erma's Cope Book* by Erma Bombeck, 1979
8. *Cosmos* by Carl Sagan, 1980
9. *A Light in the Attic* by Shel Silverstein, 1981
10. *And More by Andy Rooney* by Andy Rooney, 1982
11. *Motherhood: The Second Oldest Profession* by Erma Bombeck, 1983
12. *Iacocca: An Autobiography* by Lee Iacocca, 1984
13. *Yeager: An Autobiography* by Chuck Yeager, 1985
14. *West with the Night* by Beryl Markham, 1986
15. *Fatherhood* by Bill Cosby, 1987
16. *Gracie* by George Burns, 1988
17. *All I Really Need to Know I Learned in Kindergarten* by Robert Fulghum, 1989
18. *All I Really Need to Know I Learned in Kindergarten* by Robert Fulghum, 1990
19. *Me: Stories of My Life* by Katharine Hepburn, 1991
20. *The Autobiography of Malcolm X* by Malcolm X with Alex Haley, 1992
21. *See, I Told You So* by Rush Limbaugh, 1993
22. *Embraced by the Light* by Betty J. Eadie with Curtis Taylor

14 PEOPLE BORN ON NEW YEAR'S EVE

1. John Denver, singer/songwriter, 1943
2. Diane von Furstenberg, fashion designer, 1946
3. Sir Anthony Hopkins, movie actor, 1937
4. Val Kilmer, movie actor, 1959
5. Henri Matisse, French painter, 1869
6. Sarah Miles, movie actress, 1943
7. Pola Negri, silent screen star, 1894
8. Jule Styne, songwriter, 1905
9. Bebe Neuwirth, TV/stage actress, 1952
10. Tim Matheson, movie actor, 1948
11. Donna Summer, singer, 1948
12. Barbara Carrera, movie actress, 1945
13. Ben Kingsley, movie actor, 1943
14. George C. Marshall, U.S. general, 1880

11 PEOPLE BORN ON NEW YEAR'S DAY

1. Xavier Cugat, Cuban bandleader, 1900
2. Barry Goldwater, U.S. senator, 1909
3. J. Edgar Hoover, FBI director, 1895
4. Frank Langella, U.S. actor, 1946
5. Lorenzo de Medici, Florentine ruler, 1449
6. Paul Revere, U.S. patriot, 1735
7. Betsy Ross, U.S. seamstress, 1752
8. J. D. Salinger, U.S. writer, 1919
9. Dirk Benedict, TV actor, 1945
10. Don Novello, TV comedian, 1943
11. Dana Andrews, movie actor, 1909

8 HOLIDAYS TO CELEBRATE OTHER THAN CHRISTMAS

If you love Christmas and wish there were more days on which to celebrate, take heart! You don't have to let Christmas Eve and Christmas Day rule the month. Here are other days celebrated worldwide to honor the birth of Christ.

1. DECEMBER 6, ST. NICHOLAS DAY

    A popular holiday in Holland, Belgium, and Poland when children receive small gifts.

2. DECEMBER 12, FEAST OF OUR LADY OF GUADALUPE

    A popular religious festival in Mexico.

3. DECEMBER 13, ST. LUCIA DAY

    A popular day in Sweden when the oldest daughter wears a crown of candles and awakens her parents with breakfast.

4. DECEMBER 21, ST. THOMAS DAY

    In England, this day used to be marked by beggars seeking food for their Christmas dinner. In the rest of Europe, mischief reigned, and schoolboys often played pranks on their masters.

5. DECEMBER 23, JOHN CANOE DAY

    The start of a month-long holiday in Jamaica, during which dancing, plays, and skits are the order of the day.

6. DECEMBER 26, BOXING DAY

    In England, this official holiday is a wonderful chance to relax and have fun. It is called Boxing Day not in honor of the pugilistic sport (though, traditionally, games and sports are practiced on this day), but rather, in reference to the alms boxes in churches that were broken open so their contents could be distributed to the poor. Later, Boxing Day became a day on which one would tip servants, shop assistants, and the like.

7. JANUARY 5, TWELFTH NIGHT

    The title of one of Shakespeare's most celebrated comedies, Twelfth Night is traditionally a night of revelry to close out the end of the holiday season.

8. JANUARY 6, EPIPHANY

    The twelfth day after Christmas and traditionally celebrated as the day the Three Magi arrived in Bethlehem bearing gifts. Epiphany is a far more somber holiday than the evening that precedes it, and in the Eastern Christian churches a more important holiday than Christmas. In some countries, children receive their gifts on the Epiphany. In Italy, the kindly witch Befana (a corruption of the word *epiphany*) makes her gift-giving rounds on a broom.

6 GREAT CHRISTMAS GIFTS IN HISTORY

1. GOLD, FRANKINCENSE, AND MYRRH

    According to the Book of Matthew, magi, or wise men, came to Bethlehem bearing gifts for the Christ Child. Matthew states that the magi brought three gifts of gold, frankincense, and myrrh, which has led most people to assume that there were also three gift bringers.

2. "A VISIT FROM ST. NICHOLAS"

    In 1822, Clement C. Moore, age 42, wrote the poem "A Visit from St. Nicholas" for his six children. He read it aloud to family and friends on December 23. One guest was so enchanted with the poem that she copied it down word for word and, the following Christmas, sent it anonymously to the *Troy Sentinel*. For years, the scholarly Moore denied authorship of the poem (leading some to claim he couldn't write anything so lighthearted anyway), but finally included it in a book of his collected poems years later.

IT HAPPENED ON CHRISTMAS

3. A LIFESIZE MANGER SCENE

In 1223, St. Francis of Assisi, in attempt to make the story of Christ's birth understandable for the simple peasants he knew, constructed a manger scene in a mountainside cave near the village of Greccio. There were lifesize wooden figures, as well as oxen and ass. St. Francis invited the villagers to see his tableaux while he stood by and narrated the story.

4. "SILENT NIGHT"

It was Christmas Eve 1818 when Father Josef Mohr and church organist Franz Gruber of St. Nicholas Church in Oberndorf, Austria, realized that the church organ wasn't functioning properly. (Some say rust rendered the organ inoperable; others say mice had eaten through the bellows.) Together, they composed a simple song to be played on guitar and sung by the church choir. The song, of course, was "Silent Night," their gift to the parishioners of St. Nicholas Church.

5. THE NUTCRACKER

In 1954, Lincoln Kirstein and Morton Baum were looking for a surefire moneymaker for the fledgling New York City Ballet. Figuring that a traditional, full-length ballet was the answer, they asked ballet master and choreographer George Balanchine if he had any ideas. He immediately recalled his own childhood in Russia as a dance student, when he had danced in several productions of Tchaikovsky's *Nutcracker*. Re-creating the ballet was a labor of love for the choreographer, whose work was sometimes accused of being cold and impersonal, and he infused the production with the magic of childhood. Largely unknown to the American public, *The Nutcracker*—Balanchine's gift to the people of New York City—premiered that Christmas and was an instant hit. Every year since, the New York City Ballet has performed the ballet for the entire month of December. The ballet has also proved to be a "gift" to many regional ballet companies—by performing the ballet at Christmas, they are financially secure for the rest of the year.

6. THE NORWEGIAN CHRISTMAS TREE

Every year since World War II, in appreciation for the way the British provided a home to the exiled King Hakon, the people of Norway has sent its British friends a huge Christmas tree that is displayed with pride each year in London's Trafalgar Square.

10 PEOPLE BORN ON CHRISTMAS EVE

1. King John, English monarch, 1167
2. St. Ignatius Loyola, Roman Catholic saint, 1491
3. Kit Carson, frontiersman, 1809
4. Matthew Arnold, English poet, 1822
5. Michael Curtiz, film director, 1888
6. Howard Hughes, billionaire, 1905
7. Ava Gardner, film actress, 1922
8. Teresa Stich-Randall, opera singer, 1927
9. Mary Higgins Clark, author, 1929
10. Robert Joffrey, founder of Joffrey Ballet, 1930

10 EVENTS THAT HAPPENED ON CHRISTMAS EVE

1. 1814–The Treat of Ghent is signed, ending the War of 1812.
2. 1871–Giuseppe Verdi's opera *Aida* premieres in Cairo, Egypt.
3. 1912–Operatic soprano Luisa Tetrazzini sings on a San Francisco street corner to prove that the City by the Bay is her favorite.
4. 1943–General Dwight D. Eisenhower is appointed Commander in Chief of the Allied Forces.
5. 1943–Betty Grable is proclaimed the number one box-office attraction; Bob Hope is number two.
6. 1951–Libya is proclaimed a free and independent nation by the United Nations.

7. 1951–Gian Carlo Menotti's Christmas opera, *Amahl and the Night Visitors* premieres on NBC. It is the first opera written for television.
8. 1954–Johnny Ace, a pop singer best known for his hit "Pledging My Love," kills himself while playing Russian Roulette.
9. 1968–The spy crew of the *Pueblo* is released by North Korea after 11 months of captivity.
10. 1972–Bodybuilder Charles Atlas dies.

12 EVENTS THAT HAPPENED ON CHRISTMAS DAY

1. Year unknown–The legendary King Arthur removes the sword from the stone.
2. 1868–President Andrew Johnson grants an unconditional pardon to the former Confederate states.
3. 1898–Brooklyn and New York City merge to form the City of New York.
4. 1911–Robert Scott sets out for the North Pole.
5. 1936–Chiang Kai-shek is released, after having been kidnapped for 12 days.
6. 1942–*Ring* magazine names Sugar Ray Robinson the fighter of the year.
7. 1950–England's Stone of Scone is stolen from Westminster Abbey.
8. 1951–England's Stone of Destiny is stolen from Westminster Abbey.
9. 1965–France calls for the United States to withdraw from Viet Nam.
10. 1968–The *Apollo 8* mission returns to Earth. Astronaut Jim Lovell says, "Houston, please be informed there is a Santa Claus."
11. 1971–The Robert Redford/Paul Newman movie *The Sting* opens in New York City.
12. 1976–The Mayor of Bethlehem, Israel, receives $20,000 from Vice President Nelson Rockefeller for the maintenance of Manger Square.

IT HAPPENED ON CHRISTMAS

9 EVENTS THAT HAPPENED ON NEW YEAR'S DAY

1. 1863–President Abraham Lincoln signs the Emancipation Proclamation.
2. 1863–The U.S. Congress approves the Homestead Act, opening great areas of the American West to settlers.
3. 1902–In the first Rose Bowl, the University of Michigan beats Stanford University 45-0.
4. 1906–George M. Cohan's newest play, *45 Minutes from Broadway*, opens at New York's New Amsterdam Theatre.
5. 1946–Kathleen Wilkens of Philadelphia is born at one minute past midnight, making her the first "official" Baby Boomer.
6. 1954–Nearly 400,000 Japanese go to the Imperial Palace to sign Hirohito's guest book. In the stampede, 30 are injured and 16 are killed.
7. 1955–The National Health System goes into effect in Sweden.
8. 1959–Fidel Castro leads his army into Havana, defeating Batista and his followers.
9. 1971–Advertisements on television and radio for tobacco products are banned.

Chapter 2
The Sounds of Christmas

15 HOLIDAY SONGS WITH THE WORD "CHRISTMAS" IN THE TITLE

1. "All I Want for Christmas"
2. "The Christmas Song (Chestnuts Roasting on an Open Fire)"
3. "I'll Be Home for Christmas"
4. "It's Beginning to Look Like Christmas"
5. "White Christmas"
6. "Blue Christmas"
7. "Christmas in Killarney"
8. "Have Yourself a Merry Little Christmas"
9. "We Need a Little Christmas"
10. "We Wish You a Merry Christmas"
11. "A Holly Jolly Christmas"
12. "The Twelve Days of Christmas"
13. "Rockin' around the Christmas Tree"
14. "The Christmas Waltz"
    and, in Hawaiian . . .
15. "Mele Kalikamaka"

8 HOLIDAY SONGS THAT MENTION SANTA CLAUS IN THE TITLE

1. "Santa Claus Is Comin' to Town"
2. "I Saw Mommy Kissing Santa Claus"
3. "Here Comes Santa Claus"
4. "Santa Baby"

5. "I Believe in Santa's Cause"
6. "Santa's Beard"
7. "Be a Santa"
8. "Must Be Santa"

5 HOLIDAY SONGS WITH THE WORD "BELL" IN THE TITLE

1. "Jingle Bells"
2. "Silver Bells"
3. "I Heard the Bells on Christmas Day"
4. "Jingle Bell Rock"
5. "Carol of the Bells"

10 CAROLS WRITTEN IN THE NINETEENTH CENTURY

1. "We Three Kings of Orient Are"
2. "Silent Night"
3. "O Little Town of Bethlehem"
4. "O Holy Night"
5. "Jingle Bells"
6. "It Came upon a Midnight Clear"
7. "I Heard the Bells on Christmas Day"
8. "Good King Wenceslas"
9. "Good Christian Men Rejoice"
10. "Away in a Manger"

THE SOUNDS OF CHRISTMAS

10 CAROLS THAT DATE FROM THE RENAISSANCE OR BEFORE

1. "The Cherry Tree Carol" (medieval)
2. "God Rest You Merry, Gentlemen" (pre-16th century)
3. "Good Christian Men Rejoice" (1400s)
4. "The Holly and the Ivy" (medieval)
5. "I Saw Three Ships" (pre-15th century)
6. "O Come, O Come, Emmanuel" (12th century)
7. "O Tannenbaum" (medieval)
8. "The Twelve Days of Christmas" (medieval)
9. "We Wish You a Merry Christmas" (medieval)
10. "What Child Is This?" (pre-16th century)

3 MOVIES IN WHICH BING CROSBY SANG CHRISTMAS SONGS

1. *Holiday Inn*, "White Christmas" and "Happy Holidays"
2. *White Christmas*, "White Christmas"
3. *High Time*, "It Came upon a Midnight Clear"

4 CHRISTMAS CAROLS WRITTEN BY AMERICANS

1. "Away in a Manger" by James R. Murray
2. "O Little Town of Bethlehem" by Phillip Brooks and Lewis Redner
3. "We Thing Kings of Orient Are" by John Henry Hopkins
4. "It Came Upon a Midnight Clear" by Edmund Sears

15 PIECES OF CLASSICAL MUSIC WITH A CHRISTMAS THEME

1. Christmas Oratorio by Johann Sebastian Bach
2. L'Enfance du Christ by Hector Berlioz
3. Ceremony of Carols by Benjamin Britten
4. St. Nicholas Cantata by Benjamin Britten

5. *Pastorale dur la Naissance de Notre Seigneur Jésus Christ* by Marc-Antoine Charpentier
6. Christmas Concerto by Archangelo Corelli
7. Santa Claus Symphony by William Henry Fry
8. The Christmas Tree Suite by Franz Liszt
9. *La Nativité du Seigneur* by Oliver Messiaen
10. *Amahl and the Night Visitors* by Gian-Carlo Menotti
11. *A Christmas Carol* by Thea Musgrave
12. *Christmas Eve* by Nicolai Rimsky-Korsakov
13. *The Christmas Story* by Heinrich Schutz
14. *The Nutcracker* by Peter Ilyich Tchaikovsky
15. Fantasia on Christmas Carols by Ralph Vaughn-Williams

6 "CHRISTMAS" SONGS THAT DON'T MENTION CHRISTMAS

1. "Sleigh Ride"
2. "Winter Wonderland"
3. "Let It Snow! Let It Snow! Let It Snow!"
4. "Jingle Bells"
5. "Jingle Bell Rock"
6. "Frosty the Snowman"

15 POP STARS WHO HAVE RECORDED CHRISTMAS STANDARDS

1. "Santa Claus Is Comin' to Town" by Bruce Springsteen
2. "The Little Drummer Boy" by Bob Seeger
3. "The Little Drummer Boy" by David Bowie and Bing Crosby
4. "Do You Hear What I Hear?" by Whitney Houston
5. "Have Yourself a Merry Little Christmas" by the Pretenders
6. "Silent Night" by Dr. John
7. "I Saw Mommy Kissing Santa Claus" by John Cougar Mellencamp
8. "Winter Wonderland" by the Eurythmics
9. "The Christmas Song (Chestnuts Roasting on an Open Fire" by Ben E. King
10. "Winter Wonderland" by Aretha Franklin

11. "Jingle Bells" by Booker T. and the MGs
12. "Santa Claus Is Comin' to Town" by the Pointer Sisters
13. "We Wish You a Merry Christmas" by Peter, Paul, & Mary
14. "Silver Bells" by Wilson Pickett
15. "O Come, All Ye Faithful" by Art Garfunkel

5 CAROLS THAT BEGIN WITH "O"

1. "O Holy Night"
2. "O Come, O Come, Emmanuel"
3. "O Tannenbaum"
4. "O Little Town of Bethlehem"
5. "O Come, All Ye Faithful"

8 CHRISTMAS SONGS WRITTEN BY JOHNNY MARKS

Best known for his music for the beloved television special Rudolph the Red-Nosed Reindeer, *composer Johnny Marks has written enough holiday tunes to keep a band of carollers busy for an entire evening.*

1. "Holly Jolly Christmas"
2. "Jingle, Jingle, Jingle"
3. "The Most Wonderful Day of the Year"
4. "Rockin' around the Christmas Tree"
5. "Rudolph the Red-Nosed Reindeer"
6. "Silver and Gold"
7. "'Twas the Night before Christmas"
8. "When Santa Gets Your Letter"

THE SOUNDS OF CHRISTMAS

10 COUNTRY MUSIC CHRISTMAS SONGS AND THE STARS WHO RECORDED THEM

1. "Christmas in Dixie" by Alabama
2. "I Believe in Santa's Cause" by the Statler Brothers
3. "Christmas in My Home Town" by Charley Pride
4. "How Do I Wrap My Heart for Christmas?" by Randy Travis
5. "Country Christmas" by Loretta Lynn
6. "Pretty Paper" by Willie Nelson
7. "From Our House to Yours" by Barbara Mandrell
8. "That's What I Like about Christmas" by the Oak Ridge Boys
9. "Tennessee Christmas" by Alabama
10. "Lonely Christmas Call" by George Jones

7 CHRISTMAS SONGS INTRODUCED BY BING CROSBY

Once we heard him sing "White Christmas," it seems we couldn't get enough of Bing Crosby crooning Christmas songs. Songwriters apparently felt the same way, for Bing got first dibs at a large helping of holiday melodies.

1. "White Christmas," 1942
2. "You're All I Want for Christmas," 1948
3. "Mele Kalikamaka," 1950
4. "That Christmas Feeling," 1951
5. "It's Beginning to Look Like Christmas," 1951
6. "Sleigh Bell Serenade," 1952
7. "The Secret of Christmas," 1959

4 HOLIDAY SONGS THAT MENTION PUMPKIN PIE

1. "HOME FOR THE HOLIDAYS"

> The line reads, "I met a man who lives in Tennessee; he was headed for / Pennsylvania and some homemade pumpkin pie"

2. "OVER THE RIVER AND THROUGH THE WOODS"

   The line reads, "Hurrah for the fun, the pudding's done / Hurrah for the pumpkin pie"

3. "ROCKIN' AROUND THE CHRISTMAS TREE"

   The line reads, "Later we'll have some pumpkin pie and we'll do some carolling"

4. "SLEIGH RIDE"

   The line reads, "There's a happy feeling nothing in the world can buy / As we pass around the coffee and the pumpkin pie"

3 CHRISTMAS SONGS WITH LYRICS BY SAMMY CAHN

Lyricist Sammy Cahn won four Academy Award for his film songs ("Three Coins in the Fountain," "High Hopes," "All the Way," "Call Me Irresponsible"). He also found time to pen the words to these holiday classics.

1. "The Christmas Waltz"
2. "Let It Snow! Let It Snow! Let It Snow!"
3. "The Secret of Christmas"

THE GIFTS MY TRUE LOVE SENT TO ME FOR THE 12 DAYS OF CHRISTMAS

1. A partridge in a pear tree
2. Two turtle doves
3. Three French hens
4. Four colly birds (*Colly* is an Old English word for black; hence, four black birds—perhap ravens?)
5. Five gold rings (Many believe the word *rings* here doesn't refer to jewelry but, rather, to the gold rings around the throat of the ringed pheasant. That means that the first seven gifts are all birds!)

6. Six geese a-laying
7. Seven swans a-swimming
8. Eight maids a-milkin'
9. Nine ladies dancing
10. Ten lords a-leaping
11. Eleven pipers piping
12. Twelve drummers drumming

10 NOVELTY CHRISTMAS SONGS

1. "All I Want for Christmas (Is My Two Front Teeth)"
2. "Grandma Got Run over by a Reindeer"
3. "I Saw Mommy Kissing Santa Claus"
4. "Santa Baby"
5. "Nuttin' for Christmas"
6. "The Chipmunk Song (Christmas Don't Be Late)"
7. "Jingle Bell Rock"
8. "Rockin' around the Christmas Tree"
9. "Feliz Navidad"
10. "Suzy Snowflake"

6 SONGS THAT MENTION TOYS IN THEIR LYRICS

1. "THE CHIPMUNK SONG (CHRISTMAS DON'T BE LATE)"

    As we all know, Alvin repeatedly requests a hula hoop. However, a plane that loops the loop is also mentioned.

2. "THE MOST WONDERFUL DAY OF THE YEAR"

    A scooter and a dolly are the toys of choice in this Johnny Marks tune.

3. "JOLLY OLD ST. NICHOLAS"

   A pair of skates and a sled.

4. "UP ON THE HOUSETOP"

   A dolly, a hammer, and lots of tacks are requested.

5. "OLD TOY TRAINS"

   Roger Miller sings not only of old toy trains but also of little toy drums.

6. "IT'S BEGINNING TO LOOK LIKE CHRISTMAS"

   A pair of Hopalong boots and a pistol that shoots are listed, as well as dolls that will talk and will go for a walk.

6 POPULAR HOLIDAY SONGS ABOUT THE NATIVITY

Most popular songs—as opposed to traditional carols—are about Santa Claus, gift giving, and other picturesque descriptions of the holiday season. Now and then, though, contemporary songwriters are inspired to write about the actual events of the first Christmas.

1. "Mary's Boy Child"
2. "The Little Drummer Boy"
3. "Do You Hear What I Hear?"
4. "Rocking"
5. "Sweet Little Jesus Boy"
6. "Little Jesus, Sweetly Sleep"

4 HOLIDAY SONGS WITH THE WORD "HOME" IN THE TITLE

1. "I'll Be Home for Christmas"
2. "(There's No Place Like) Home for the Holidays"
3. "Christmas in My Home Town"
4. "Hurry Home for Christmas"

5 SONGS YOU PROBABLY KNOW ALL THE WORDS TO

1. "Silent Night"
2. "White Christmas"
3. "Rudolph the Red-Nosed Reindeer"
4. "Jingle Bells"
5. "Santa Claus Is Comin' to Town"

9 SONGS THAT LENT THEIR TITLES TO MOVIES OR TELEVISION SPECIALS

1. "RUDOLPH THE RED-NOSED REINDEER"

    The television classic that fleshes out the story of Rudolph to include an elf who wants to be a dentist and an entire island of misfit toys.

2. "FROSTY THE SNOWMAN"

    A popular cartoon shown each Christmas, featuring the voice of Jackie Vernon as Frosty.

3. "SANTA CLAUS IS COMIN' TO TOWN"

    A television Christmas perennial that tells the "true" story of how red-haired Kris Kringle became Santa Claus. Among the revelations: Mrs. Claus' first name is Jessica.

4. "WHITE CHRISTMAS"

   The song was such a hit in 1942's *Holiday Inn* that 12 years later they decided to do an entire movie based on the idea of snow at Christmas. A classic with Bing Crosby, Danny Kaye, Vera-Ellen, and Rosemary Clooney.

5. "IT CAME UPON A MIDNIGHT CLEAR"

   A 1984 television film starring Mickey Rooney as a dead detective who wants to return to earth to spend Chistmas with his grandson.

6. "HOME FOR THE HOLIDAYS"

   An unjolly 1972 television film starring Walter Brennan, Julie Harris, Jessica Walter, and Sally Field. Brennan's daughters return home to kill his young wife.

7. "SILENT NIGHT"

   In slightly altered form, everyone's favorite carol lent its name to the 1969 television film *Silent Night, Lonely Night* starring Lloyd Bridges and Shirley Jones.

8. "HERE COMES SANTA CLAUS"

   This 1984 film had a little boy named Simon trading his toy chest for the safe return of his parents.

9. "A MIDNIGHT CLEAR"

   This 1992 World War II film tells the story of an encounter between American GIs and their German counterparts.

3 NON-HOLIDAY MOVIES OR PLAYS THAT INTRODUCED NEW CHRISTMAS SONGS

1. *MAME*

    This blockbuster of the 1966 Broadway season centered on the adventures of zany Auntie Mame, played by *Murder She Wrote*'s Angela Lansbury. When the stock market crashes and things look bad, she belts out the cheery "We Need a Little Christmas," written by Jerry Herman.

2. *PROMISES, PROMISES*

    This 1968 Broadway hit, a musical reworking of the Academy Award-winning film *The Apartment*, featured songs by the hot songwriting team of Burt Bacharach and Hal David. Jerry Ohrbach starred and won a Tony for best actor. Among the tunes: "I'll Never Fall in Love Again," "Promises, Promises," and "Christmas Day," a holiday song.

3. *MEET ME IN ST. LOUIS*

    A lovely, sentimental movie directed by Vincente Minnelli. The episodic plot features a year in the life of the Smith family of St. Louis. Judy Garland sings the classic "Have Yourself a Merry Little Christmas" to her depressed little sister, played by Margaret O'Brien.

5 SONGS THAT IDEALIZE WINTER WEATHER

Once Christmas is over, snow seems to lose its considerable power to charm us. But these songs manage to make the prospect of Jack Frost nipping at your nose and folks dressed up like Eskimos sound like fun.

1. "White Christmas"
2. "Winter Wonderland"
3. "Let It Snow! Let It Snow! Let It Snow!"
4. "Sleigh Ride"
5. "The Christmas Song (Chestnuts Roasting on an Open Fire)"

YOU'D BE SURPRISED—7 STARS WHO HAVE RECORDED CHRISTMAS SONGS

1. "Santa Baby" by Madonna
2. "Merry Christmas, Baby" by Ike and Tina Turner
3. "Santa Claus Goes Straight to the Ghetto" by James Brown
4. "Late in December" by Jackie Gleason
5. "The Little Drummer Boy" by Marlene Dietrich
6. "Wreck the Halls with Boughs of Holly" by the Three Stooges
7. "Santa Claus and His Old Lady" by Cheech and Chong

4 CAROLS THAT MENTION ANGELS IN THE TITLE

1. "Angels We Have Heard on High"
2. "Angels, from the Realms of Glory"
3. "Hark! The Herald Angels Sing"
4. "Songs of Praise the Angels Sing"

4 SPIRITUALS ABOUT CHRISTMAS

1. "Go Tell It on the Mountain"
2. "Rise Up, Shepherd, and Follow!"
3. "Mary Had a Baby"
4. "Sister Mary Had But One Child"

5 CAROLS ORIGINALLY SUNG IN LATIN

1. "O Come, O Come, Emmanuel"
2. "O Come All Ye Faithful" ("Adeste Fideles")
3. "Of the Father's Love Begotten"
4. "On This Day Earth Shall Ring"
5. "Unto Us a Boy Is Born" ("Puer Noblis")

NAMES MENTIONED INCIDENTALLY IN 7 CHRISTMAS SONGS

1. **MISS FANNY BRIGHT**

   In the second verse of "Jingle Bells," a first-person narrator is introduced ("A day or two ago / I thought I'd take a ride"), who tells us that he is going to take "Miss Fanny Bright" for a ride in his one-horse open sleigh.

2. **PARSON BROWN**

   In the song "Winter Wonderland" the enamored couple builds a snowman and promptly names him Parson Brown. Apparently, this snowman then offers to marry them.

3. **FARMER GRAY**

   In the song "Sleigh Ride" the perfect ending to a perfect day is the birthday party at Farmer Gray's.

4. **JACK FROST**

   He is the culprit, of course, "nipping at your nose" in "The Christmas Song" ("Chestnuts Roasting on an Open Fire").

5. **NELLIE, SUZY, JOHNNY**

   Three of the children mentioned in the song "Jolly Old St. Nicholas." Suzy wants a sled, Johnny wants skates, and Nellie likes yellow, blue, and red.

6. **LITTLE NELL AND BILL**

   In the song "Up on the Housetop," Little Nell would like her stocking to be filled with a doll. Bill would like a hammer, tacks, a whistle, a ball, and a set of jacks.

7. JOHNNY, TOMMY, AND SUSIE

>Three of the children the narrator of the song "Nuttin' for Christmas" terrorizes. He breaks a bat over Johnny's head, makes Tommy eat a bug, and ties a knot in Susie's hair.

6 NON-CHRISTMAS MOVIES IN WHICH CHRISTMAS SONGS WERE SUNG (AND BY WHOM)

1. "Have Yourself a Merry Little Christmas" sung by Judy Garland in *Meet Me in St. Louis*
2. "Christmas Story" sung by Doris Day in *On Moonlight Bay*
3. "Silent Night" sung by Deanna Durbin in *Lady on a Train*
4. "Merry Christmas" sung by Judy Garland in *In the Good Old Summertime*
5. "The Secret of Christmas" sung by Bing Crosby in *Say One for Me*
6. "It Came upon a Midnight Clear" sung by Bing Crosby in *High Time*

5 VERY OLD SECULAR CAROLS

Not all ancient carols were religious in nature, nor is Irving Berlin soley responsible for concentrating on the celebratory aspects of Christmas. Here are five very old carols that focus on eating, drinking, and being merry.

1. "Deck the Halls"
2. "Here We Come a-Wassailing"
3. "The Twelve Days of Christmas"
4. "We Wish You a Merry Christmas"
5. "The Boar's Head Carol"

10 TRADITIONAL CAROLS THAT DESCRIBE THE NATIVITY

1. "The First Noel"
2. "Away in a Manger"
3. "Silent Night"
4. "O Come All Ye Faithful"
5. "What Child Is This?"
6. "O Little Town of Bethlehem"
7. "It Came upon a Midnight Clear"
8. "Hark! The Herald Angels Sing"
9. "We Three Kings of Orient Are"
10. "Joy to the World"

9 CAROLS OF BRITISH ORIGIN

1. "The First Noel"
2. "God Rest You Merry, Gentlemen"
3. "Deck the Halls"
4. "The Coventry Carol"
5. "The Holly and the Ivy"
6. "Here We Come a-Wassailing"
7. "Good King Wenceslas"
8. "What Child Is This?"
9. "Hark! The Herald Angels Sing"

3 CAROLS FROM FRANCE

1. "O Holy Night"
2. "Angels We Have Heard on High"
3. "He Is Born" ("Il Est Ne")

9 CHRISTMAS SONGS THAT KIDS LOVE

1. "Rudolph the Red-Nosed Reindeer" by Johnny Marks
2. "Up on the Housetop" by B. R. Hanby
3. "Jingle Bells" by James Pierpont
4. "Here Comes Santa Claus" by Gene Autry and Oakey Haldeman
5. "Frosty the Snowman" by Steve Nelson and Jack Rollins
6. "The Chipmunk Song" ("Christmas Don't Be Late") by Ross Bagdasarian
7. "All I Want for Christmas (Is My Two Front Teeth)" by Don Gardner
8. "Jolly Old St. Nicholas" Traditional
9. "Santa Claus Is Coming to Town" by Haven Gillespie and J. Fred Coots

9 CAROLS WITH UNUSUAL TITLES

1. "The Friendly Beasts" Traditional French
2. "The Cowboy Carol" by Cecil Broadhurst and Frances Root Hadden
3. "The Workers' Carol" by Paul Petrocokino and Morris Martin
4. "Come, My Dear Old Lady" Traditional Spanish
5. "The Farmers' Carol" by Paul Petrocokino and Edward Devlin
6. "What Is This Perfume So Appealing?" Traditional French
7. "Baloo, Lammy" Traditional Scottish
8. "Pat-a-Pan" Traditional French
9. "Fum, Fum, Fum" Traditional Spanish

7 LITTLE-KNOWN INTERNATIONAL CAROLS

1. "The Christmas Nightingale" Traditional German
2. "Shepherds, Up!" Traditional Austrian
3. "Whence, O Shepherd Maiden?" Traditional French
4. "Carol of the Bagpipers" Traditional Italian
5. "The Donkey Carol" Traditional English
6. "Mary the Virgin to Bethlehem Went" Traditional Swedish
7. "Shepherds, Come A-Running" Traditional Polish

CHRISTMAS AROUND THE COUNTRY

Courtesy of Greater North Michigan Avenue Association

Silhouetted against the December sky, Chicago's Water Tower is surrounded by a medley of Christmas lights.

Courtesy of Peter J. Schulz/City of Chicago

The lights and decorated windows at Chicago's Marshall Field's attract holiday shoppers to State Street.

CHRISTMAS AROUND THE COUNTRY

Courtesy of San Francisco Convention and Visitors Bureau

At San Francisco's Ghirardelli Square, home to the great chocolate maker, a giant Christmas tree takes center stage during the holidays.

CHRISTMAS AROUND THE COUNTRY

Courtesy of Louisville and Jefferson County Convention and Visitors Bureau

A performer dressed in Victorian garb brings Christmas cheer to the Dickens on Main celebration in Louisville, Kentucky, which features strolling carolers, food, and music.

Courtesy of Eureka/Humboldt County Convention and Visitors Bureau

The Carson Mansion--one of Eureka, California's Victorian treasures--was once home to lumber baron William Carson and is decorated to the hilt every Christmas season.

CHRISTMAS AROUND THE COUNTRY

Courtesy of New York Convention and Visitors Bureau

Immortalized in the 1947 film *Miracle on 34th Street*, New York's Macy's Thanksgiving Day Parade has become an American holiday tradition.

CHRISTMAS AROUND THE COUNTRY

Courtesy of New York Convention and Visitors Bureau

The holidays wouldn't be as festive in New York City without the famous Christmas tree that stands majestically over the skating pond at Rockefeller Center.

CHRISTMAS AROUND THE COUNTRY

Courtesy of Convention and Visitors Bureau of Kansas City

Country Club Plaza boasts one of the most spectacular lighting displays in the country: 200,000 lights are illuminated every Thanksgiving night over a 14-block area, ringing in the holiday season in Kansas City, Missouri.

Courtesy of Colonial Williamsburg Foundation

A blanket of snow adds a holiday touch to Williamsburg's famed historic district.

Courtesy of Colonial Williamsburg Foundation

Tourists enjoy the annual lighting of the Yule Log in the heart of Williamsburg's historic district.

Courtesy of Preservation Society of Newport County

Capturing the magic of a Gilded Era Christmas, the library at Newport, Rhode Island's Breakers mansion is decked with a Victorian tree and vintage toys.

CHAPTER 3
FROM PAGE TO SCREEN TO STAGE

14 THINGS ST. NICK DOES IN "THE NIGHT BEFORE CHRISTMAS"

In the 56 brief lines of his poem "A Visit from St. Nicholas" (popularly known as "The Night Before Christmas") author Clement C. Moore paints St. Nick as a very active senior citizen. Here's everything he does in his short visit.

1. Whistles
2. Shouts
3. Calls his reindeer by name
4. Comes down the chimney with a bound
5. Holds the stump of his pipe tight in his teeth
6. Laughs, causing his belly to shake like a bowful of jelly
7. Winks his eye
8. Nods his head
9. Fills all the stockings
10. Turns with a jerk
11. Lays his finger aside of his nose
12. Gives another nod
13. Goes up the chimney
14. Exclaims, "Happy Christmas to all and to all a good night!"

FROM PAGE TO SCREEN TO STAGE

9 FILMED VERSIONS OF A CHRISTMAS CAROL

It's a good thing the copyright expired long ago on Dickens' classic tale: moviemakers have been dipping into this beloved classic for inspiration for many years now. Sometimes the interpretations are quite literal, other times only the bare bones of the original story are retained. One thing's for certain, though: audiences love Ebenezer Scrooge!

1. *A CHRISTMAS CAROL*

    Starring British actor Seymour Hicks, this little-known 1933 version is prized by aficionados for Hicks' especially crotchety portrayal of Scrooge.

2. *A CHRISTMAS CAROL*

    With Reginald Owen as Scrooge, this 1938 version plays up some of the supporting characters. Scrooge's nephew, Fred, is seen attending church and Bob Cratchit (played by an ebullient Gene Lockhart) is spied sliding on ice. Ann Rutherford, who played one of Scarlett O'Hara's sisters in *Gone with the Wind*, is here cast as the Ghost of Christmas Past.

3. *A CHRISTMAS CAROL (aka SCROOGE)*

    Perhaps the version most often televised, due to Alastair Sim's sneering, toothy portrayal of the title character in this 1951 release.

4. *SCROOGE!*

    This all-singing, all-dancing version is very much in the tradition of the British musical *Oliver!* Albert Finney overacts a bit as Scrooge, but it's an infectious portrayal nonetheless. Bob Cratchit is here portrayed as a handsome young father rather than a middle-aged man.

5. *MR. MAGOO'S CHRISTMAS CAROL*

    The cantakerous voice of Jim Backus as Mr. Magoo makes this animated version something of a minor classic. Jack Cassidy provides the voice of Bob Cratchit, and there are a few cute tunes thrown in as well (provided by Jule Style of *Gypsy* fame).

6. MICKEY'S CHRISTMAS CAROL

   Walt Disney Studios pulled some of its most famous stock characters out of storage for this animated reworking of Dickens' fable. Scrooge McDuck (Donald's irascible uncle) played Scrooge, Mickey was Bob Cratchit, and Goofy a rather surprising choice as the ghost of Jacob Marley.

7. A CHRISTMAS CAROL

   This television version was a production of the Hallmark Hall of Fame and was a class act all the way around. George C. Scott is the lovable miser, portraying him as a somewhat more elegant figure than we're accustomed to. Susannah York gave a delicately shaded performance as Mrs. Cratchit.

8. SCROOGED!

   A very updated version, with Bill Murray taking the role of Scrooge. In this incarnation, Scrooge is a jaded television executive. Carol Kane is memorable as a high-energy ghost with a penchant for violence.

9. A MUPPET CHRISTMAS CAROL

   The latest entry in the *Christmas Carol* sweepstakes was this 1992 holiday offering from the folks at Disney, feauring the versatile Michael Caine as Scrooge and a bevy of Jim Henson's smiling Muppets.

FROM PAGE TO SCREEN TO STAGE

SANTA'S 8 REINDEERS AS NAMED BY CLEMENT C. MOORE

Before Clement C. Moore's poem "A Visit from St. Nicholas" became so popular it wasn't widely assumed that Santa was transported by reindeer. Some had him walking his route; others thought he rode a horse or drove a wagon. Once Clement C. Moore put names to all those reindeers, though, the world fell in love with them.

1. Blitzen
2. Comet
3. Cupid
4. Dancer
5. Dasher
6. Donner
7. Prancer
8. Vixen

5 TELEVISION CHRISTMAS SPECIALS PRODUCED BY RANKIN & BASS

1. Frosty the Snowman
2. The Little Drummer Boy
3. The Little Drummer Boy, Book II
4. Rudolph the Red-Nosed Reindeer
5. Santa Claus Is Comin' to Town

13 CHRISTMAS MOVIES OF THE LAST 12 YEARS (1983–94)

Though there hasn't been a true classic (like 1947's Miracle on 34th Street) in many years, that hasn't stopped movie makers from tackling the subject of Christmas. Of course, there have been a fair share of television movies, too, but these are some of the more well-known theatrical releases.

1. A Christmas Story, 1983
2. Mickey's Christmas Carol, 1983

3. One Magic Christmas, 1985
4. Scrooged! 1988
5. National Lampoon's Christmas Vacation, 1989
6. Prancer, 1990
7. Home Alone, 1990
8. A Muppet Christmas Carol, 1993
9. Home Alone II, 1993
10. George Balanchine's The Nutcracker, 1993
11. The Nightmare Before Christmas, 1993
12. The Santa Clause, 1994
13. Miracle on 34th Street, 1994

10 ANIMATED CHRISTMAS SPECIALS PRODUCED FOR TELEVISION

1. Yes, Virginia, There Is a Santa Claus
2. 'Twas the Night before Christmas
3. Frosty the Snowman
4. Rudolph the Red-Nosed Reindeer
5. Noël
6. The Little Drummer Boy
7. The Little Drummer Boy, Book II
8. A Charlie Brown Christmas
9. Santa Claus Is Comin' to Town
10. Mr. Magoo's Christmas Carol

14 THINGS THE GRINCH STOLE (BESIDES CHRISTMAS) IN THE BOOK *HOW THE GRINCH STOLE CHRISTMAS*

1. The stockings all hung in a row
2. Pop guns
3. Bicycles
4. Roller skates
5. Drums
6. Checkerboards
7. Tricycles

8. Popcorn
9. Plums
10. Who-pudding
11. Roast beast
12. The last can of Who-hash
13. The Christmas tree
14. The log for the fire

5 REALLY DOWNBEAT CHRISTMAS MOVIES

Not every holiday film is full of the mirth and cheer that characterize such classics as White Christmas and Miracle on 34th Street. Even if they do have happy endings, these five films seem to be full of more than their share of Christmas gloom.

1. ONE MAGIC CHRISTMAS

   Mary Steenburgen starred in this 1985 film about a family struggling to make ends meet. While Steenburgen struggles to find a few affordable Christmas gifts for her children and her husband tries to convince her that they should open a bicycle shop, an angel (played by Harry Dean Stanton) sends Steenburgen's daughter on a magical trip to the North Pole. In spite of this, the overall effect is quite depressing.

2. SILENT NIGHT, LONELY NIGHT

   Shirley Jones and Lloyd Bridges starred in this 1969 made-for-television movie about two unhappily married people who come together at a New England inn at Christmas. The TV movie was an adaptation of a 1959 Broadway play by Robert Anderson starring Henry Fonda and Barbara Bel Geddes.

3. *MEET JOHN DOE*

   In this Frank Capra classic, Barbara Stanwyck plays a journalist who concocts a letter from "John Doe" stating that he is so depressed over the Christmas season, he will commit suicide by jumping from the roof of City Hall. The letter receives such widespread attention that she is forced to hire a man (Gary Cooper) to be her John Doe. Things come to a head when Cooper's character, disillusioned by the way the world treats "John Doe" really does try to kill himself on Christmas Eve.

4. *THE CHRISTMAS TREE*

   William Holden and Verna Lisi starred in this 1969 tearjerker about a father trying to make his son's last days (the boy is suffering from leukemia caused by radiation) happy ones. In true Hollywood fashion, the child dies on Christmas Eve.

5. *BLACK CHRISTMAS*

   Surely a first: a holiday slasher film. The former star of *Romeo and Juliet*, Olivia Hussey, starred with Margot Kidder, and John Saxon in this "thriller" about a series of bizarre murders committed in a sorority house on Christmas Eve.

9 CHRISTMAS CLASSICS AND THE ACADEMY AWARDS THEY DID OR DIDN'T WIN

Just because it's a holiday favorite doesn't mean it's considered a cinema classic. The films we love to watch on television every holiday season didn't often make it to the winner's circle at Oscar time.

1. *Miracle on 34th Street*—3 (including one for Edmund Gwenn's perfect portrayal of Kris Kringle)
2. *Holiday Inn*—1 (for its song "White Christmas")
3. *A Christmas Story*—0
4. *White Christmas*—0
5. *A Christmas Carol* (1951)—0
6. *It's a Wonderful Life*—0

7. *Going My Way*—7 (including Oscars for its stars, Bing Crosby and Barry Fitzgerald)
8. *A Christmas Carol* (1938)—0
9. *Christmas in Connecticut*—0

10 DISNEY CHARACTERS WHO "STARRED" IN MICKEY'S CHRISTMAS CAROL

1. Scrooge McDuck—Ebenezer Scrooge
2. Mickey Mouse—Bob Cratchit
3. Goofy—Jacob Marley
4. Donald Duck—Fred
5. Jiminy Cricket—The Ghost of Christmas Past
6. Willie the Giant—The Ghost of Christmas Present
7. Pete—The Ghost of Christmas Yet to Come
8. Daisy Duck—Isobel
9. Minnie Mouse—Mrs. Cratchit
10. Mr. Toad—Fezziwig

4 VARIATIONS ON THE "SCROOGE" THEME

Anytime you see a holiday movie in which a character is transformed by the magical power of Christmas, you can be sure the writers have been influenced by Dickens' Christmas Carol. Here are a few works that borrow this popular theme.

1. *HOW THE GRINCH STOLE CHRISTMAS*

   He's mean, he's nasty, and he hates Christmas. He even has a name as memorable as Scrooge's. Dr. Seuss' wonderful creation, however, stands on his own as a wonderfully memorable Yuletide grouch.

2. **IT'S A WONDERFUL LIFE**

   This one is a bit more complex. Frank Capra has bisected Scrooge. There's his basically good side (George Bailey) and his mercenary side (Henry Potter). George almost falls prey to his weaker side several times: he almost takes a job from Potter and then he gives up on life, convinced everyone would be better off "if I'd never been born." In place of four ghosts, Capra gives us one angel, the gentle-voiced Clarence. And in the end, George's Christmas spirit gets the upper hand when he says, "I want to live again."

3. **AN AMERICAN CHRISTMAS CAROL**

   Henry Winkler dispensed with his leather jacket for this 1979 television movie in which he portrayed hard-as-nails American financier Benedict Slade. David Wayne co-starred.

4. **SCROOGED!**

   Bill Murray plays a cold-hearted television executive (who produces some really bad shows) who's evilness was apparently caused by a troubled childhood (judging by the flashback sequences). Alfre Woodard as his secretary is a Bob Cratchit for the 1980s: a single working mother. With a little help from some friendly spirits, even this cynical trashmonger learns to see the beauty in life.

6 REASONS GEORGE BAILEY NEVER LEAVES BEDFORD FALLS IN *IT'S A WONDERFUL LIFE*

1. After high school graduation, George can't afford to go to college. He has to work four years at the Bailey Bros. Building & Loan to save up tuition money.

2. Shortly before he's to leave for college, his father has a fatal stroke. The board of the Bailey Bros. Building & Loan votes to keep the company open only if George stays on as secretary.

3. George's brother, Harry, gets a job offer from his father-in-law. George insists that Harry take the job, rather than coming to work for the Building & Loan, as they had planned.

4. On the day he and Mary are supposed to leave for their honeymoon, there is a run on the bank and George is forced to face his shareholders and pay them money out of his own pocket.

5. While his friends go off to serve in World War II, George is classified 4-F because of his bad ear and is forced to stay stateside.

6. When Mr. Potter offers him a job that would involve several trips each year to New York, he realizes he can't live with himself if he works for Potter.

4 STARS KNOWN FOR THEIR CHRISTMAS TELEVISION SPECIALS

1. ANDY WILLIAMS

   Back in the 1960s, Andy Williams was synonomous with Christmas. His annual television specials showcased lots of pretty winter scenery and the breathy singing of his then-wife, Claudine Longet. Andy often featured the Osmond Brothers, his discoveries, on these specials.

2. PERRY COMO

   Perry Como's Christmas specials were notable because they were in a different location each year. Perry showed us how Christmas was celebrated in such far-flung locales as London, New Mexico, and Paris. The show always ended with Perry singing "O Holy Night."

3. BOB HOPE

   Bob's specials have always featured a monologue, some skits, and whatever young starlet Bob fancied that year (Brooke Shields was a particular favorite). His Christmas specials are also a showcase for the two college football teams who will be participating in the Rose Bowl. Viewers also get a sneak peak at the Rose Queen and her court.

4. BING CROSBY

Surely the most beloved of all Christmas television specials were Bing Crosby's. Like Andy Williams' specials, Bing included his family for singing and skits. Perhaps the most memorable guest star on his specials was David Bowie, who appeared on Bing's last special in 1976. Viewers across the nation waited for the end of these specials, when Bing sang his signature tune, "White Christmas."

15 STARS WHO HAVE LENT THEIR VOICES TO ANIMATED CHRISTMAS SPECIALS

1. Jim Backus in *Mr. Magoo's Christmas Carol*
2. Roger Miller in *Nestor, the Long-Earred Donkey*
3. Fred Astaire in *Santa Claus Is Comin' to Town*
4. Red Skelton in *Rudolph's Shiny New Year*
5. Mickey Rooney in *Santa Claus Is Comin' to Town*
6. Walter Matthau in *The Stingiest Man in Town*
7. Zero Mostel in *The Little Drummer Boy*
8. Greer Garson in *The Little Drummer Boy*
9. Shelley Winters in *Frosty's Winter Wonderland*
10. Andy Griffith in *Frosty's Winter Wonderland*
11. Buddy Hackett in *Jack Frost*
12. Art Carney in *Leprechaun's Christmas Gold*
13. Burl Ives in *Rudolph the Red-Nosed Reindeer*
14. Boris Karloff in *How the Grinch Stole Christmas*
15. Jackie Vernon in *Frosty the Snowman*

12 MISFITS IN THE TELEVISION SPECIAL RUDOLPH THE RED-NOSED REINDEER AND WHY THEY'RE MISFITS

1. Rudolph, the legendary red-nosed reindeer
2. Herbie, the elf who wanted to be a dentist
3. Yukon Cornelius, the prospector for silver and gold who *always* came up empty-handed
4. A Jack-in-the-Box named Charlie
5. Nesting clowns with a wind-up mouse inside
6. A spotted elephant
7. A train with square wheels
8. A water pistol that shoots jelly
9. A bird that can't fly—it swims
10. A cowboy who rides an ostrich
11. A boat that sinks
12. A doll. We're never quite sure *why* she's on the Island of Misfit Toys, as she seems perfectly fine. Nevertheless, she definitely considers herself a misfit. Perhaps she suffers from low self-esteem.

3 HOLIDAY ENTERTAINMENTS STARRING FRED ASTAIRE

1. *HOLIDAY INN*

    Fred played a dancer named Ted Hanover in this lovable holiday film directed by Mark Sandrich and co-starring Mr. Christmas himself, Bing Crosby.

2. *SANTA CLAUS IS COMIN' TO TOWN*

    In this animated television special, Fred supplied the voice of the narrator/mailman. The animated figure of the mailman was also the spittin' image of the lantern-jawed dancer.

3. *THE MAN IN THE SANTA CLAUS SUIT*

    This 1979 holiday film co-starring Gary Burghoff featured Fred as a costume shop owner. In addition to playing seven characters in the movie, Fred also found time to sing the movie's title song.

5 CHRISTMAS MOVIES THAT TAKE PLACE PARTLY IN NEW ENGLAND

1. *Christmas in Connecticut* (Connecticut)
2. *White Christmas* (Vermont)
3. *Holiday Inn* (Connecticut)
4. *Little Women* (Massachusetts)
5. *One Magic Christmas* (Massachusetts)

10 CHRISTMAS MOVIES THAT TAKE PLACE PARTLY IN NEW YORK CITY

1. *Santa Claus: The Movie*
2. *Miracle on 34th Street*
3. *Christmas in Connecticut*
4. *Home Alone II*
5. *The Lemon Drop Kid*
6. *Meet John Doe*
7. *Going My Way*
8. *Holiday*
9. *The Cheaters*
10. *Tenth Avenue Angel*

THE 9 HOLIDAYS FEATURED IN THE MOVIE *HOLIDAY INN* AND THE IRVING BERLIN SONGS THAT ACCOMPANY THEM

When Bing Crosby's character in Holiday Inn comes up with the crazy idea of running an inn open only on holidays, he says he'll be open 15 days a year. Unfortunately, the movie only shows us these 9 holidays. We'll just have to guess what the other holidays were—perhaps Arbor Day?

1. New Year's Eve ("Happy Holidays")
2. Lincoln's Birthday ("Abraham")
3. Valentine's Day ("Be Careful, It's My Heart")
4. Washington's Birthday ("I Can't Tell a Lie")
5. Easter Sunday ("Easter Bonnet")
6. Independence Day ("Let's Say It with Firecrackers")
7. Thanksgiving ("I've Got Plenty to Be Thankful For")
8. Christmas ("White Christmas")
9. New Year's Eve ("Let's Start the New Year Right")

4 OPERAS WITH CHRISTMAS SCENES

1. *LA BOHEME* BY GIACOMO PUCCINI

   Though the opera isn't about Christmas, its famous opening scene, when the poet Rodolfo falls in love with the seamstress Mimi in his garrett dwelling, takes place on Christmas Eve. Later, the lovers go to the Café Momus where the toy vendor, Parpignol, is selling gifts to those last-minute Parisian shoppers.

2. WERTHER BY JULES MASSENET

   The story of the poet Werther and his unrequited love for his best friend's wife, Charlotte. As the opera opens, a group of children is being taught a Christmas carol. Later in the opera, Werther returns to Charlotte after a long absence, and she tells him she will always remain with her husband. In despair, Werther shoots himself, dying in Charlotte's arms after she finally admits she loves him. Meanwhile, the voices of children offstage sing the Christmas carol they learned earlier.

3. *AMAHL AND THE NIGHT VISITORS* BY GIAN CARLO MENOTTI

   This opera tells the story of the journey of the Wise Men and Amahl, the crippled child they meet along the way. When Amahl's mother tries to steal the gold intended for the Christ Child to help her own son, the Wise Men prove remarkably understanding. Amahl then offers to bring his sole possession—his crutch—as a gift to the Christ Child. To everyone's amazement, Amahl now finds that he can walk unaided and he sets off into the night with the Wise Men.

4. *A CHRISTMAS CAROL* BY THEA MUSGRAVE

   This modern-day British opera has a libretto by its female composer, Thea Musgrave. The opera follows Dickens book quite closely and was originally produced for London's Sadler's Wells Theatre.

3 BEVERAGES THAT DANCE FOR CLARA IN THE NUTCRACKER

Once the Nutcracker and Clara cross the border to the Kingdom of Sweets in Tchaikovsky's ballet The Nutcracker, *Clara is treated to a performance of dancing flowers and the Sugarplum Fairy. Three beverages also come to life, each representing their country of origin.*

1. Chocolate (Spain)
2. Coffee (Arabia)
3. Tea (China)

5 NON-CHRISTMAS MOVIES WITH MEMORABLE CHRISTMAS SCENES

1. Young at Heart
2. Meet Me in St. Louis
3. Little Women
4. The Cheaters
5. Desk Set

4 GHOSTS WHO VISITED SCROOGE

1. JACOB MARLEY

   Scrooge's former business partner. He lets Scrooge know that Scrooge is getting this last chance due solely to his (Marley's) intervention. Scrooge replies, with uncharacteristic politeness, "You were always a good friend to me . . . Thank'ee!"

2. THE GHOST OF CHRISTMAS PAST

   "A strange figure—like a child: yet not so like a child as like an old man." Takes Scrooge on a journey through his own childhood and youth, which first starts to melt the old miser's heart.

3. THE GHOST OF CHRISTMAS PRESENT

   "A jolly Giant" surrounded by food and carrying a torch with which he dispenses good will. He could easily be mistaken for Father Christmas. Scrooge visits the homes of Bob Cratchit and his nephew, Fred, and is also taken on an around-the-world voyage—even to a ship at sea—to see how Christmas is celebrated.

4. THE GHOST OF CHRISTMAS YET TO COME

   Dickens refers to this Ghost as "the Phantom." Hooded in black, he never speaks, but shows Scrooge a dreary vision of the future.

7 SONGS BING CROSBY SINGS IN *WHITE CHRISTMAS*

1. "Blue Skies"
2. "Count Your Blessings"
3. "Mandy"
4. "Snow"
5. "What Do You Do with a General?"
6. "White Christmas"
7. "I Wish I Was Back in the Army"

10 CHRISTMAS POEMS BY 10 GREATS OF BRITISH LITERATURE

1. "A Christmas Carol" by G. K. Chesterton
2. "Journey of the Magi" by T. S. Eliot
3. "The Oxen" by Thomas Hardy
4. "Yule Log" by Robert Herrick
5. "Moonless Darkness Stands Between" by Gerard Manley Hopkins
6. "Christmas" by Leigh Hunt
7. "Eddi's Service" by Rudyard Kipling
8. "A Ballad for Christmas" by Walter de la Mare
9. "Heap on More Wood" by Walter Scott
10. "Ghost Story" by Dylan Thomas

10 CHRISTMAS TALES BY CHARLES DICKENS OTHER THAN *A CHRISTMAS CAROL*

1. "The Chimes"
2. "A Christmas Tree"
3. "The Cricket on the Hearth"
4. "Going into Society"
5. "The Holly-Tree"
6. "A Message from the Sea"
7. "The Poor Relation's Story"
8. "The Schoolboy's Story"
9. "Tom Tiddler's Ground"
10. "What Christmas Is as We Grow Older"

FROM PAGE TO SCREEN TO STAGE

6 CHRISTMAS CLASSICS FROM CHILDREN'S LITERATURE

1. *THE POLAR EXPRESS* BY CHRIS VAN ALLSBURG

    In this beautifully illustrated modern-day classic, a boy is taken on a magical ride aboard the Polar Express, a train that takes him to the North Pole. Santa Claus lets the boy choose one gift to take with him, and the boy chooses a bell from the reindeers' harness. But when he returns home, he discovers that only those who believe in Santa Claus can hear the bell ring.

2. *THE SNOWMAN* BY RAYMOND BRIGGS

    This lovely, wordless picture book tells the story of a magical snowman who takes a boy on a flight across Christmas morning skies.

3. *THE STORY OF HOLLY AND IVY* BY RUMER GODDEN

    A girl and her doll are the main characters in this tender story. Ivy is an orphan, Holly is a doll left in a shop window on Christmas Eve, and Mr. and Mrs. Jones are a childless couple. All the elements of this story come together for a classic happy ending.

4. *HOW THE GRINCH STOLE CHRISTMAS* BY DR. SEUSS

    Everyone knows this Dr. Seuss story in which the Grinch fails to steal Christmas in spite of his best (or worst, depending on your point of view) efforts.

5. *BABAR AND FATHER CHRISTMAS* BY JEAN DE BRUNHOFF

    In this Yuletide adventure Babar, the elephant king, finds Father Christmas on behalf of his children. He persaudes the old man to take time off and rest in elephant's country. In return for this much-needed vacation, Father Christmas gives Babar a magical red suit that will allow him to play Father Christmas to all the little elephants in the Elephants' country.

6. *THE NUTCRACKER* BY E. T. A. HOFFMAN

This is the classic story that is the basis for the Tchaikovsky ballet. It tells of Marie; her mysterious godfather, Herr Drosselmeyer; and her adventures with the Nutcracker. A beautifully illustrated edition by Maurice Sendak has found a new audience for this old tale

15 MURDER MYSTERY NOVELS THAT TAKE PLACE AT CHRISTMAS

1. *Benjamin Franklin and a Case of Christmas Murder* by Robert Lee Hall
2. *Christmas at Candleshoes* by Michael Innes
3. *An English Murder* by Cyril Hare
4. *Gone to the Dogs* by Susan Conant
5. *A Holiday for Murder* (also known as *Murder for Christmas* and *Hercule Poirot's Christmas*) by Agatha Christie
6. *Tied up in Tinsel* by Ngaio Marsh
7. *The Twelve Deaths of Christmas* by Marian Babson
8. *The Christmas Crimes at Puzzel Manor* by Simon Brett
9. *Upon Some Midnight Clear* by K. C. Constantine
10. *'Tis the Season to be Dying* by Alisa Craig
11. *A Carol in the Dark* by Cathleen Jordan
12. *Rest You Merry* by Charlotte MacLeod
13. *Corpus Christmas* by Margaret Maron
14. *Merry Christmas, Murdock* by Robert J. Ray
15. *Maigret's Christmas* by Georges Simenon

MEMORABLE CHRISTMAS GIFTS IN 7 WORKS OF LITERATURE

1. "THE GIFT OF THE MAGI" BY O. HENRY

   A young couple without much money tries to find a way to buy the perfect gift for one another. Jim sells his watch to buy a comb for Della's beautiful hair, while she cuts off and sells her hair to buy a chain for his watch.

2. *LITTLE WOMEN* BY LOUISA MAY ALCOTT

   The March girls all find a way to buy "Marmee," their mother, the perfect Christmas gift on their very limited budget. Amy buys her a bottle of cologne (selfish Amy originally bought Marmee the smallest and cheapest bottle but exchanged it for a big bottle early Christmas morning), Jo gives her slippers, Beth gives her handkerchiefs, and Meg gives her a pair of gloves. Marmee, in turn, gives each of her daughters a copy of the life of Christ, each bound in a different color leather. Later in the day, the entire family gives their Christmas breakfast to a poor German family.

3. *LITTLE HOUSE IN THE BIG WOODS* AND *LITTLE HOUSE ON THE PRAIRIE* BY LAURA INGALLS WILDER

   In the children's classic, *Little House in the Big Woods*, all the cousins receive red mittens and a stick of peppermint candy. Being the youngest, the book's heroine, Laura, also receives a rag doll. In *Little House on the Prairie*, she again receives a stick of candy but also receives a new tin cup, a heart-shaped cake, and a penny.

4. *THE NUTCRACKER* BY E. T. A. HOFFMAN

   The book's heroine, Marie Stahlbaum, receives a doll with numerous accessories and a silk dress. Her brother, Fritz, receives a hobby horse and toy soldiers (specifically, Hussars) in red and gold with silver sabers. The famed nutcracker is brought to the party by Marie's godfather for all the children to enjoy, but Marie likes the nutcracker best.

FROM PAGE TO SCREEN TO STAGE

5. *A CHILD'S CHRISTMAS IN WALES* BY DYLAN THOMAS

   Poet Thomas' touching Christmas memories (which are available in a splendid edition illustrated by Trina Schart Hyman) divide Christmas gifts into two categories to which all children can relate: useful and useless. The dull, useful gifts include mufflers, mittens, and pictureless books. The far more desirable useless gifts are such things as jelly babies, a tram conductor's cap, a little hatchet, troops of bright tin soldiers, and toffee and fudge.

6. *A CHRISTMAS CAROL* BY CHARLES DICKENS

   At the begining of the story, Scrooge unwillingly gives Bob Cratchit the day off for Christmas. At the end of the book, the reformed Scrooge bestows upon the Cratchit family a splendid turkey and a raise in salary.

7. *GONE WITH THE WIND* BY MARGARET MITCHELL

   During the war, Scarlett O'Hara painstakingly removes the embroidery from a gaudy shawl given to her by Rhett Butler in order to make a fine gold sash to complement Ashley Wilkes' Confederate uniform.

5 CLASSIC CHRISTMAS FILMS RELEASED BY PARAMOUNT STUDIOS

Hollywood's Paramount Studios was founded in 1914 by Adolph Zukor. The studio was primarily known for its light family fare, which may explain why it was so good at producing Christmas classics like these.

1. *Christmas in July*, 1940
2. *Holiday Inn*, 1942
3. *Going My Way*, 1944
4. *The Lemon Drop Kid*, 1951
5. *White Christmas*, 1954

FROM PAGE TO SCREEN TO STAGE

11 REASONS WE BELIEVE KRIS KRINGLE IS REALLY SANTA CLAUS IN THE MOVIE *MIRACLE ON 34th STREET*

1. He knows the correct order of the reindeer and gently corrects the man who is setting up plastic reindeer in a store window.

2. He knows how to crack a whip and tries to show Macy's drunken Santa Claus the correct way to do it.

3. He owns his own Santa Claus suit, which is a real beauty.

4. He has a real beard, not the kind that wraps around his ears.

5. He speaks Dutch to a little Dutch girl who comes to see him at Macy's.

6. According to little Susan Walker, "he's so kind and jolly."

7. On his employment application, he lists his next of kin as Dasher, Dancer, and all the other reindeer.

8. On his employment application, he lists his birthplace as the North Pole.

9. The U.S. Post Office—an official branch of the U.S. government—delivers its Santa Claus mail to Kris at the courthouse.

10. He makes sure that Fred and Doris drive past Susan's dream house—presumably so that they will get married and buy it for her.

11. Once they enter the house, Susan proclaims that it is just as she imagined, right down to the swing in the backyard. To further underline the point that Kris is responsible for this happiness, a cane that looks just like his is leaning against the fireplace mantel.

5 CHILDREN IN CHRISTMAS STORIES WHO ARE KIND OF SAD

Although children are supposed to be at their happiest at Christmas, the Christmas literature is full of children who are melancholy, lonely, or just plain poor. Luckily, most of these stories have happy endings.

1. THE LITTLE MATCH GIRL

   In Hans Christian Andersen's story, the little girl who sells matches is poor and unloved, except for the memory of her beloved grandmother. Rather then selling matches on Christmas Eve, the little girl lights all of them to keep warm, though she fears that her parents will be angry. Sadly, her efforts to keep warm fail, and she dies of the cold.

2. TINY TIM

   Surely no Christmas child is more sad than little Tiny Tim in *A Christmas Carol*. Crippled and walking with a crutch (though we are never told why), it is his plight—shown to Scrooge by the Ghost of Christmas Present—that persuades the old miser that Bob Cratchit is more than a clerk. Scrooge, in a sudden change of heart, says, "Tell me spirit, will Tiny Tim live?" At the end of the story, Dickens tells us that, in time, Scrooge became like a second father to Tiny Tim.

3. YOUNG SCROOGE

   Scrooge himself is pictured as a melancholy child in the memories shown to him by the Ghost of Christmas Past. Alone and abandoned at his boarding school, he is the only child—year after year—whose father doesn't want him home for Christmas. Young Ebenezer thus retreats into a world of his own, surrounded by books, especially *Tales of the Arabian Nights*, which is his favorite. During his teen years, his older sister, Fan, comes to get him at Christmas, declaring that "Father is so much kinder than he used to be." Perhaps he, too, was visited by ghosts?

4. IVY

In Rumer Godden's classic children's tale, *The Story of Holly and Ivy*, six-year-old Ivy is a melancholy orphan. Since the orphanage where she lives closes down for the holidays, she is supposed to go to its sister orphanage in the country. But Ivy is convinced that her "grandmother" is waiting for her in Appleton, a town along the tracks. She gets off the train in Appleton and begins wandering around the town. Meanwhile, in Mr. Blossom's toy shop, a beautiful Christmas doll named Holly remains unpurchased on Christmas Eve, and the long-childless Mrs. Jones dreams not only of that pretty doll (who also catches Ivy's eye), but of a little girl to play with her. All these lonely people come together on Christmas Eve for a happy ending. An animated version was televised in 1991 as *The Wish That Changed Christmas*.

5. SALLY WHO

In *How the Grinch Stole Christmas*, the Grinch's nocturnal activities awaken little Sally Who, who, visibly upset, wants to know why "Santa Claus" is stealing her family's Christmas tree. The Grinch smoothly tells a lie to Sally, who is easily placated and sent back to bed.

4 CHRISTMAS FILMS OF THE SILENT SCREEN ERA

1. *The Night Before Christmas*, 1905
2. *The Christus*, 1917
3. *The Night Before Christmas*, 1926
4. *Babes In Toyland*, 1924

5 REALLY OFFBEAT CHRISTMAS FILMS

1. *I'LL BE SEEING YOU*, 1944

    In this unusual Ginger Rogers vehicle, she plays a convict home on parole for the holidays who falls for a shell-shocked soldier, played by Joseph Cotten.

2. *CHRISTMAS HOLIDAY*, 1944

    In this decidedly unsuccessful attempt to change its two stars' images, wholesome Deanna Durbin plays a nightclub singer who marries a murderer, played by Gene Kelly. He goes to jail, and though she helps him escape, he attempts to kill her anyway. He is killed in the process.

3. *BUSH CHRISTMAS*, 1947

    This Australian release tells the story of children trying to capture wily horse thieves on Christmas Eve.

4. *SANTA CLAUS CONQUERS THE MARTIANS*, 1964

    In this classic "B" picture, Santa Claus is kidnapped by Martians in order to give their kids the Christmas they've always dreamed of (apparently, the little Martians watch Earth television and have learned about Santa). One of the Martians, Dropo, gets so into the spirit of things that the real Santa Claus names Dropo Santa Claus to the Martians so that he can get himself back to all the good little kiddies on Earth.

5. *THE NIGHTMARE BEFORE CHRISTMAS*, 1993

    From producer Tim Burton (*Beetlejuice, Batman*) came this weird, stop-action animated film. Jack Skellington is the bored Pumpkin King of Halloween Town looking for a new holiday to celebrate. With the help of a loyal rag doll named Sally, he discovers the secrets of Christmas Town and Santa Claus. Though this musical film had an eerie look, its message was upbeat.

29 MADE-FOR-TELEVISION CHRISTMAS MOVIES AND THE YEAR THEY AIRED

1. Silent Night, Lonely Night, 1969
2. The Homecoming, 1971
3. Home for the Holidays, 1972
4. Miracle on 34th Street, 1973
5. A Dream for Christmas, 1973
6. Young Pioneers' Christmas, 1976
7. The Gathering, 1977
8. It Happened One Christmas, 1977
9. Sunshine Christmas, 1977
10. Christmas Miracle in Caulfield, U.S.A., 1977
11. The Nativity, 1978
12. A Christmas to Remember, 1978
13. Christmas Lilies of the Field, 1979
14. An American Christmas Carol, 1979
15. A Christmas without Snow, 1980
16. The Gift of Love: A Christmas Story, 1983
17. The Night They Saved Christmas, 1984
18. Christmas Eve, 1986
19. The Christmas Gift, 1986
20. The Christmas Star, 1986
21. Christmas Comes to Willow Creek, 1987
22. A Very Brady Christmas, 1988
23. The Christmas Wife, 1988
24. It Nearly Wasn't Christmas, 1989
25. Christmas on Division Street, 1991
26. The Story Lady, 1991
27. In the Nick of Time, 1991
28. A Christmas Romance, 1994
29. One Christmas, 1994

Chapter 4
Christmas Around the World

WHO BRINGS THE GIFTS IN 25 NATIONS

1. Austria—Krampus
2. Belgium—Saint Nicholas
3. Brazil—Papa Noël
4. Bulgaria—Grandfather Koleda
5. Chile—Viejo Pascuero (Old Man Christmas)
6. Costa Rica—Christ Child
7. England—Father Christmas
8. Finland—Father Christmas
9. Germany—Christkind Angel
10. Guatemala—Christ Child
11. Holland—Sinter Klaas
12. Hungary—Mikulas
13. Italy—Befana or Babbo Natale
14. Japan—Hoteiosho
15. Lebanon—Magic Mule
16. Mexico—The Three Wise Men
17. Norway—Julenisse
18. Poland—Star Man
19. Russia—Babouschka or Grandfather Frost
20. Spain—The Three Wise Men
21. Sweden—Jultomte the Gnome
22. Switzerland—Christkind
23. Syria—The Smallest Camel in the Wise Men's Caravan
24. United States—Santa Claus
25. Wales—Father Christmas

HOW TO SAY "MERRY CHRISTMAS" IN 16 DIFFERENT NATIONS

1. Denmark—Glaedelig Jul
2. England—Merry Christmas
3. France—Joyeux Noël
4. Germany—Fröhliche Weinachten
5. Greece—Kala Christougena
6. Holland—Zalig Kerstfeest
7. Italy—Buon Natale
8. Japan—Meri Kurisumasu
9. Mexico—Feliz Navidad
10. Norway—Gledelig Jul
11. Poland—Wesolych Swiat
12. Portugal—Boas Festas
13. Romania—Sarbatori Vesele
14. Spain—Felices Pascuas
15. Sweden—Glad Jul
16. Wales—Nadolog Llawen

CHRISTMAS FISH DISHES SERVED IN 7 COUNTRIES

1. Austria—Carp
2. Czechoslvakia—Deviled carp
3. France—Oysters
4. Italy—Capitone (eel)
5. Hungary—Jellied carp
6. Sweden—Lutfisk (carp in a cream sauce)
7. United States (Deep South)—Oyster stew

7 POPULAR HOLIDAY BEVERAGES

1. Ale Posset—A punch made with milk, ale, beer, wine, and spices; it is popular in Yorkshire, England.

2. Eggnog—The famed American holiday drink is a frothy mixture of sugar, egg, and cream.

3. Glögg—This popular Swedish mulled wine is served warm with almonds and raisins.

4. Gluhwein—Austrians enjoy this hot, spiced wine on Christmas.

5. Lamb's Wool—Another English specialty, this one made with apples, ales, and spices.

6. Syllabub—Also known as milk punch, this is a popular Christmas beverage in the American South.

7. Wassail—This popular English punch (surely the only beverage that has inspired its own carol, "Here We Come A-Wassailing"), is a tasty combination of ale and spices.

CHRISTMAS DESSERTS SERVED IN 7 COUNTRIES

1. Czechoslovakia—Masika (fruit stew)
2. England—Christmas (plum) pudding or mince pies
3. France—Bûche de Noël
4. Germany—Lebkuchen and Pfeffernüsse
5. Italy—Torrone molle
6. Spain—Turrón (a nougat made of almonds in a caramel syrup)
7. United States—fruitcake

CHRISTMAS BREADS SERVED IN 6 COUNTRIES

1. Chile—Pan de pasqua
2. Czechoslovakia—Calta (braided bread) and Vanochka
3. Germany—Stollen
4. Greece—Christopsomo
5. Italy—Panettone
6. Sweden—Julekake

6 CHRISTMAS BIRDS SERVED IN 7 COUNTRIES

1. Capon—Italy
2. Goose—Austria, Denmark, France (Alsace)
3. Peacock—Renaissance through Victorian England
4. Pheasant—United States (Deep South), England
5. Swan—Renaissance England
6. Turkey—England, France (Burgundy), Spain, United States

WHERE THE GIFTS ARE LEFT IN 8 COUNTRIES

1. Belgium—Small baskets
2. Brazil—Shoes
3. Ecuador—Shoes in the window
4. England—Stockings
5. France—Shoes
6. Sicily—Stockings
7. Spain—Shoes left on the balcony
8. United States—Under the tree

THE CENTER OF CHRISTMAS CELEBRATIONS IN 7 COUNTRIES

1. Armenia—An olive branch
2. Brazil—Manger scene
3. Costa Rica—Manger scene
4. Germany—Christmas tree

5. Italy—Yule log
6. New Zealand—Christmas tree
7. United States—Christmas tree

HOW CHILDREN IN 6 COUNTRIES CIRCULATE THEIR CHRISTMAS LISTS

1. DENMARK

    Danish children send their letters to Santa Claus in Greenland.

2. ENGLAND

    English children write their letters and then toss them in the fireplace. If a draft carries the letter up the chimney, the children believe the list will be fulfilled by Father Christmas.

3. FINLAND

    Finnish children believe that their Father Christmas lives in Lapland on Korvantunturi hill, and they send their letters to him there.

4. ITALY

    Children place their "Christmas Letter" under their father's dinner plate on Christmas Eve. Since gifts aren't exchanged until January 6, there is plenty of time for the list to be read and fulfilled.

5. PANAMA

    In Panama, children charmingly send their letters to Baby Jesus in Heaven c/o St. Peter.

6. UNITED STATES

    American children traditionally send their lettters to Santa Claus at the North Pole, where he resides with his wife and eight reindeer (nine, if you count Rudolph).

WHEN GIFTS ARE EXCHANGED IN 12 COUNTRIES

1. Armenia—January 19
2. Belgium—December 6
3. England—December 25
4. Ethiopia—January 7
5. Holland—December 5
6. Italy—January 6
7. Mexico—January 6
8. Poland—December 7 and December 24
9. Puerto Rico—December 25 and January 6
10. Spain—January 5
11. Sweden—December 24
12. United States—December 24 or December 25

WHO ASSISTS THE GIFT BRINGER IN 6 COUNTRIES

1. Austria—Krampus accompanies St. Nicholas.
2. Czechoslovakia—The Devil (Cert), carrying whips and chains, accompanies St. Nicholas.
3. Finland—A straw goat, Ukko, brings Father Christmas.
4. Germany—Pelznickle or Ru-Klas accompanies the Christkind.
5. Holland—Black Peter accompanies St. Nicholas.
6. Switzerland—Schmutzli, the Black One, accompanies Samichlaus.

IMPORTANT YULETIDE HOLIDAYS (OTHER THAN CHRISTMAS) IN 11 COUNTRIES

1. Bulgaria—Nova Godina (January 1)
2. England—Boxing Day (December 26)
3. Holland—Second Christmas Day (December 26)
4. Ireland—Little Christmas (January 6)
5. Norway—Dirty Sunday (the last Sunday before Christmas)

6. Philippines—December 16 (when Christmas officially begins)
7. Poland—St. Nicholas Day (December 6)
8. Puerto Rico—Bethlehem Day (January 1)
9. Scotland—Hog Manay (January 1) and Handsel Monday (first Monday of the New Year)
10. Sweden—January 13 (when the Christmas season ends)
11. Syria—December 4 (when Christmas season begins)

WHEN 3 GROUPS CELEBRATE CHRISTMAS IN BETHLEHEM

Each year, the city of Bethlehem—and more particularly, Manger Square—is the center of Christmas celebrations. But because different groups of Christians celebrate on different dates, the celebrations in Bethlehem go on for almost a month.

1. DECEMBER 24

    Catholics and Protestants hold their masses and services on this day, with some activity continuing on Christmas Day.

2. JANUARY 6

    The Greek Orthodox Church has always held Epiphany, the date on which it maintains Christ was baptised, to be a more important date than Christmas.

3. JANUARY 19

    The Armenian church also honors Epiphany, but since is operates on the old Julian calendar, this date falls on January 19.

HOW HEADS OF STATES (AND MINOR OFFICIALS) PARTICIPATE IN CHRISTMAS IN 4 COUNTRIES

1. UNITED STATES

    In 1923, President Coolidge started the tradition of the National Community Christmas Tree, lighting it on Christmas Eve. In the

1950s, President Eisenhower moved the date up to December 17 (where it remains today) so that the tree could be enjoyed even longer. During the Iran hostage crisis in the 1980s, President Carter opted to only light the star at the top of the tree. Presidents also send out an official Christmas card each year, the most famous of which is probably the photograph of Caroline Kennedy's pony, Macaroni, pulling her across the snow-covered White House lawn in a sleigh.

2. UNITED KINGDOM

It's a tradition for patriotic Britons to gather around the radio on Christmas day and listen to the monarch's Christmas address.

3. FINLAND

In Helsinki, the mayor announces the start of Christmas at midnight on Christmas Eve. He also reminds his countrymen to go to church the next day.

4. HOLLAND

In Amsterdam, the mayor and other civic leaders participate in the famous St. Nichola parade. The parade ends at the Royal Palace, where the Royal Family greets St. Nicholas, riding atop an elegant white horse. St. Nicholas then asks any children in the Royal Family if they've been good boys and girls.

HOW CHRISTMAS IS CELEBRATED IN 7 NON-CHRISTIAN COUNTRIES

1. CHINA

Less than one percent of China's population is Christian, but they get into the full spirit of the holiday, hanging out stockings, waiting for Santa Claus, and—in true Chinese fashion—setting off fireworks. They refer to the holiday as the Holy Birth Festival.

CHRISTMAS AROUND THE WORLD

2. GREENLAND

   Among the native Indians of Greenland, there is much singing on Christmas Day. Trees are imported and decorated, and gifts are usually handmade of such native materials as sealskin and tusks. Christmas also acts somewhat as a Sadie Hawkins day, for on this day, men serve women.

3. HONG KONG

   Christmas cards, written in Chinese characaters, are sent, and churchgoing is a popular activity. Santa Claus is called Nice Old Father or Christmas Old Man. Even in Hong Kong, Santa Claus travels via reindeer.

4. INDIA

   In rural areas simple gifts such as food are exchanged. In the cities, Christmas is more commercialized, though gift giving, tipping, and charity are major activities. Long church services are the order of the day, and poinsettias are often used as decorations.

5. IRAN

   In Iran, Christians refer to Christmas as Little Festival (Easter is Big Festival). The holiday is preceded by an entire month of fasting, during which no meat or dairy products are eaten.

6. JAPAN

   Only about 500,000 Japanese are Christians. Christmas here is very much along American guidelines with greeting cards and shopping dominating the scene. Chartitable work and donations are also part of the Christmas activities.

7. PAKISTAN

   December 25 is a national holiday already, in honor of Pakistan's founder, Jinnah. Among Christians—who call the holiday "Big Day"—visits to family and friends are customary, as is the exchange of gifts.

Chapter 5
A Holiday Potpourri

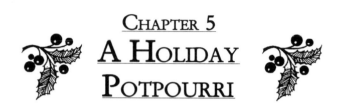

8 TRENDY CHRISTMAS GIFTS AND THEIR YEARS OF PEAK POPULARITY

1. Teddy Bear, 1903
2. The Coonskin Cap, 1955
3. Hula Hoop, 1957
4. Skateboard, 1965
5. Pet Rock, 1974
6. Cabbage Patch Doll, 1984
7. Barney the Dinosaur, 1993
8. Power Rangers, 1994

6 FAMOUS CHRISTMAS TREES

1. The melancholy tree in Hans Christian Andersen's short story "The Fir Tree"
2. The tree that stands year 'round in Christmas, Florida.
3. The first tree set up in the White House by Franklin Pierce, 1854.
4. The first tree set up on the White House lawn by Calvin Coolidge, 1923.
5. The national Christmas tree that the president lights every year in Washington, D.C.
6. The tree Norway sends each year to London's Trafalgar Square in appreciation for England's friendship during World War II.

10 ITEMS YOU SEE AT THE GROCERY STORE MORE OFTEN AT CHRISTMAS

1. Candy canes
2. Fruitcakes
3. Eggnog
4. Hams
5. Turkeys
6. Hershey's Kisses in red and green foil
7. Bulk nuts (in the produce section)
8. Pumpkin pie filling
9. Apple cider
10. French fried onions (for all those casseroles)

7 PRESIDENTS WHO WERE IN OFFICE FEWER THAN 4 CHRISTMASES

1. William Henry Harrison—0
2. James Garfield—0
3. Zachary Taylor—1
4. Warren G. Harding—2
5. John F. Kennedy—2
6. Millard Fillmore—3
7. Gerald Ford—3

16 PRESIDENTS WHO WERE IN OFFICE FOR ONLY 4 CHRISTMASES

1. John Adams
2. John Quincy Adams
3. Martin Van Buren
4. John Tyler
5. James Polk
6. Franklin Pierce
7. James Buchanan
8. Abraham Lincoln
9. Andrew Johnson
10. Rutherford B. Hayes

11. Chester Arthur
12. Benjamin Harrison
13. William Henry Taft
14. Herbert Hoover
15. Jimmy Carter
16. George Bush

16 PRESIDENTS WHO WERE IN OFFICE FOR MORE THAN 4 CHRISTMASES

1. Richard M. Nixon—5
2. Calvin Coolidge—6
3. Lyndon B. Johnson—6
4. George Washington—8
5. Thomas Jefferson—8
6. James Madison—8
7. James Monroe—8
8. Andrew Jackson—8
9. Ulysses S. Grant—8
10. Grover Cleveland—8
11. Theodore Roosevelt—8
12. Woodrow Wilson—8
13. Harry S Truman—8
14. Dwight D. Eisenhower—8
15. Ronald Reagan—8
16. Franklin D. Roosevelt—12

A HOLIDAY POTPOURRI

7 STATES WITH CITIES CALLED BETHLEHEM

1. Connecticut
2. Georgia
3. Indiana
4. Kentucky
5. Maryland
6. New Hampshire
7. Pennsylvania

4 COUNTRIES WITH CITIES CALLED BETHLEHEM

1. Israel
2. New Zealand
3. South Africa
4. Wales

4 TIMES YOU'LL FIND THE WORD "CHRISTMAS" ON A WORLD GLOBE

1. Christmas Island—An island in the Pacific Ocean where nuclear testing was done.
2. The Christmas Islands—A chain of islands in the Indian Ocean.
3. Christmas Hills—A hilly ridge in Tasmania.
4. Christmas Ridge—A underwater land mass in the Pacific Ocean.

17 AMERICAN TOWNS WITH CHRISTMAS-Y NAMES

1. Christmas, Michigan
2. Christmas, Missouri
3. Christmas Cove, Maine
4. Christmas Valley, Oregon
5. Fort Christmas, Florida
6. Holly, Colorado
7. Holly, Michigan
8. Holly, West Virginia

9. Mistletoe, Kentucky
10. Mount Holly, New Jersey
11. Mount Holly, Vermont
12. Noel, Missouri
13. Noel, Virginia
14. Santa Claus, California
15. Santa Claus, Idaho
16. Santa Claus, Indiana
17. Snowflake, Arizona

2 CHRISTMAS DISHES THAT CONTAIN NO PLUMS

We're not sure what it is about Christmas and plums, but the fruit turns up in more recipe names than it does in the actual lists of ingredients.

1. PLUM PUDDING

    The traditional English dessert contains plenty of dried fruit and suet, but no plums.

2. SUGARPLUMS

    We all know the line "While visions of sugarplums danced through their heads," but how many of us actually know what sugarplums are? In fact, they're generally taken to be round or oval chocolates filled with nougats or creams. In fact, sugarplums are the basic boxed candy we're used to seeing at Valentine's Day.

HOW 3 LAWS AFFECTED CHRISTMAS DAY

1. 1541—England's Unlawful Game Act declares that archery is the only sport to be played on Christmas Day.

2. 1644—Oliver Cromwell's Puritan government forbids the celebration of Christmas in any form.

3. 1659—The General Court of Massachusetts makes the celebrating of Christmas a penal offense.

4 ITEMS YOU FIND IN THE CHRISTMAS PUDDING AND THEIR MEANINGS

English tradition dictates that the cook throw these items into the Christmas pudding as she's stirring the pot. When the pudding is served, everyone hopes they'll be one of the lucky recipients of a coin or a ring.

1. Button—Bachelorhood
2. Coin—Wealth
3. Ring—Marriage
4. Thimble—Spinsterhood

4 SOURCES FOR OUR POPULAR IMAGE OF SANTA CLAUS

1. WASHINGTON IRVING

    In his *Knickerbocker History* the author of "The Legend of Sleepy Hollow" took St. Nick out of the realm of religious figures and into the realm of folklore. It was Irving who had St. Nicholas flying over the city in a wagon to deliver gifts to children.

2. CLEMENT C. MOORE

    Moore wrote "A Visit from St. Nicholas," with its magical opening line, "'Twas the night before Christmas" solely for the entertainment of his children. A family friend was so impressed with the poem that she sent it to a newspaper to be published, where it was an instant hit. Moore added a lot to the Santa Claus folklore. His biggest contribution was naming those eight reindeer. He also established Santa's playful, elfish qualities.

3. THOMAS NAST

In his day, Victorian illustrator Nast was known primarily as a political cartoonist, but his memorable pictures of a smiling St. Nick have kept his name alive. Nast captured perfectly the twinkling eyes, rosy cheeks, and plump belly of Moore's description. And he almost always pictured St. Nick accompanied by a bag overflowing with toys.

4. COCA-COLA COMPANY

The full-color advertisements that the Coca-Cola Company produced beginning in the 1930s (and expertly painted by Haddon Sundblom) added one important element to our image of Santa Claus. Sundblom dispensed with Moore's description of a "right jolly old elf," making his Santa Claus a veritable giant. Sundblom is also responsible for Santa's red suit—as you may recall, Moore had St. Nick dressed "all in fur from his head to his foot."

THE 3 KINGS AND THEIR OFFICIAL TITLES

1. Balthazaar—King of Ethiopia
2. Caspar—King of Tarsus
3. Melchior—King of Arabia

5 PLANTS ASSOCIATED WITH CHRISTMAS AND THEIR MEANINGS

1. EVERGREEN

A symbol of undying life and, therefore, associated with Christ. As with so many Christmas tradition, the decking of our homes with evergreens was originally a pagan tradition to celebrate the winter solstice.

2. HOLLY

> The red of the holly berry has traditionally been symbolic of Christ's blood. This plant is also associated with the crown of thorns that Christ wore at the Crucifixion.

3. MISTLETOE

> At one time, it was belived that the Cross was made from the wood of mistletoe. The tradition of kissing under the mistletoe is a pre-Christian tradition popularized by the usually stoic English

4. POINSETTIA

> Mexican legend says that a young boy who could not afford to bring a gift to the crèche knelt to offer a prayer instead. The poinsettia (or the Flower of the Night as it is called in Mexico) grew where the boy had knelt. The poinsettia was introduced to the United States by John Henry Poinsett.

5. ROSE

> For a rose to grow in winter is as miraculous as for the Son of God to be born in a humble manger. That is the legend associated with this Christmas plant.

7 CHRISTMAS TRADITIONS REVIVED OR POPULARIZED BY THE VICTORIANS

Charles Dickens wasn't the only Victorian crazy about Christmas. It seems that everyone in the nineteenth century, particularly the English and Americans, wanted to make sure that Christmas was a holiday rivaled by no other. Not many of us realize just how many of our holiday traditions have been around only for the last 100 years or so.

1. THE CHRISTMAS CARD

> Popularized by Louis Prang, a German printer who developed an

inexpensive method of printing in color. Early Christmas cards looked a lot like Valentines, which they emulated. Within a few years though, wintertime scenes and pictures of Santa Claus had replaced the hearts and flowers.

2. THE CHRISTMAS TREE

Queen Victoria's German spouse, Prince Albert, brought the Teutonic tradition of a decorated tree to England with him. When a popular magazine of the day, *Illustrated News*, printed a picture of Albert, Victoria, and their children around a Christmas tree every English housewife worth her plum pudding wanted a tree as well. A similar etching in an American magazine several years later set off Christmas tree fever on this side of the Atlantic.

3. *A CHRISTMAS CAROL*

Charles Dickens is often credited with single-handedly reviving Christmas with the publication of his short novel *A Christmas Carol*. After Oliver Cromwell's Puritan govenment banned Christmas in 1644, the holiday was never celebrated quite as lustily as it had been in earlier times. With the warm, joyous picture of Christmas that Dickens painted, everyone wanted to celebrate Christmas. *A Christmas Carol* has been a hit since day one.

4. SANTA CLAUS

For good or for bad, the overriding image across the world of the gift bringer is a jolly man in a red velvet suit, and this image largely stems from the work of two Americans, author Clement C. Moore ("A Visit from St. Nicholas") and illustrator Thomas Nast. Before the Victorian era, the mythical St. Nicholas was more of a religious figure, very much inspired by the real-life bishop who was his namesake.

5. CHRISTMAS CAROLS

Though the Victorians didn't invent Christmas carols, they certainly brought them back to life. In *A Christmas Carol*,

Dickens depicts a boy singing the old medieval carol "God Rest You Merry, Gentlemen." Perhaps the strongest catalyst to reviving old carols (and composing new ones) was the 1871 publication of *Christmas Carols Old and New*. English Victorians made organized carolling—going from door to door for the simple joy of singing—a popular activity.

6. CHRISTMAS CRACKERS

Popular in England for more than 100 years, crackers are becoming equally popular in the United States, where they can be found in a wide variety of mail-order catalogs. They were invented in 1860 when a confectioner added a small explosive to his wrapped candies in order that they might "pop" when opened. Over time, the crackers (so named because of the sound they make when opened) evolved into a cardboard tube filled with any number of treats and trinkets. In fact, many crackers today contain no candy at all.

7. GIFT GIVING

Around the time that mail-order catalogs and department stores such as Sears Roebuck were taking the country by storm, so did widespread, expensive gift giving. Merchants advertised their wares with trade cards, in newspaper ads, and from shop windows. Children of well-to-do middle-class parents could now ask Santa Claus for toy soldiers, expensive train sets, and porcelains dolls for Christmas. The era of commericalized gift giving was here, and retail merchants have been rubbing their hands gleefully ever since.

9 TOYS THAT NEVER GO OUT OF STYLE

1. Balls
2. Building blocks
3. Dolls
4. Guns
5. Marbles
6. Sleds
7. Teddy bears
8. Toy trains
9. Wagons

5 TREES THAT MAKE GOOD CHRISTMAS TREES

1. DOUGLAS OR FRASIER FIR

    The fir tree holds its needles well once cut. It was immortalized in Hans Christian Andersen's poignant short story "The Fir Tree."

2. BALSAM FIR

    Known for its classic conical shape, it is easy to decorate.

3. RED CEDAR

    A fragrant juniper known for its red wood and dark green, overlapping needles.

4. PINE

    A handsome, long-needled tree with a "chubby" shape.

5. SPRUCE

    Also cone-shaped like the fir tree, this coniferous tree has a trim, neat shape.

3 POPULAR TREE TRIMS AND THEIR ORIGINS

1. GARLAND

    Decking a tree with garland has less-than-picturesque origins. It is said that Germanic pagans would decorate trees on the outskirts of their war camps with the intestines of their enemies. Later, pre-Christian midwinter festivities in what was to become Germany centered on a garland-bedecked tree.

2. LIGHTS

    The legend says that religious reformer Martin Luther was walking through the forest one evening and was taken with the beauty of the stars shining through the branches of the evergreens. He was so taken with the sight that he went home and decked a tree with candles to duplicate the effect.

3. ORNAMENTS

    The staggering variety of ornaments we see on a tree today were originally simple glass balls, and these, in turn, evolved from the tradition of decking an evergreen tree with fruit. In medieval Germany "paradise trees"—evergreens decked with apples—were the focal point of religious plays used to explain the story of Adam and Eve to illiterate peasants. The paradise tree in time evolved into the decorated Christmas tree.

WHAT THE 4 WEEKS OF ADVENT SYMBOLIZE

To children, the four weeks of advent merely mean opening up the doors on the advent calendar and waiting for the presents to come. But to the church, the four weeks symbolize the four ways Christ has made himself visible to man.

1. Week 1: In the flesh
2. Week 2: In the hearts of his believers
3. Week 3: At the death of every man
4. Week 4: On the Day of Judgment

THE ANNIVERSARY YEARS OF 12 IMPORTANT CHRISTMAS TRADITIONS

1. 350 A.D.

    Pope Julius I officially establishes December 25 as the day on which to celebrate Christ's birth.

2. 1818

    The song "Silent Night" is composed by Franz Gruber and Josef Mohr.

3. 1822

    Clement C. Moore writes "A Visit from St. Nicholas" ("The Night Before Christmas") as a Christmas gift for his children.

4. 1827

    The first of illustrator Thomas Nast's famous pictures of Santa Claus—picturing a jolly, rotund fellow smoking a pipe—is published.

5. 1843

    Charles Dickens' great novel *A Christmas Carol* is published and is credited with single-handedly restoring the Christmas spirit in England.

6. 1843

    The first Christmas card, a secular design featuring people sitting around a dining room table, is designed by J. C. Horsley for the printer Henry Cole. It sells only moderately well.

7. 1846

    The Illustrated News publishes a picture of Queen Victoria and her family standing around a Christmas tree. This homey image inspires British housewives to emulate the Royal Family and heralds a new popularity for Christmas trees, which had previously been a mostly German tradition. Two years later, the American magazine *Godey's Lady Book* publishes a similar picture, and Christmas tree fever hits America.

8. 1863

Free city postal delivery is established in the United States, helping to spur the growth of the fledgling Christmas card industry.

9. 1871

In England, the book *Christmas Carols Old and New* is published, bringing to light many forgotten medieval carols and making "Christmas carolling" door-to-door a common practice.

10. 1872

The first Sears Roebuck catalog is released, starting the great American tradition of mail-order shopping for Christmas.

11. 1942

The song "White Christmas" by Irving Berlin is introduced in the movie *Holiday Inn.*

12. 1962

The U.S. Post Office issues its first Christmas stamp.

8 HOLIDAY SUPERSTITIONS AND MYTHS

1. If you meet someone under the mistletoe, you have to kiss them.

2. On Christmas Eve, oxen kneel and cattle speak.

3. If you eat plum pudding, pay attention to what's baked inside. If you find a button in your serving, it indicates bachelorhood. A coin means wealth, a ring means marriage is in the offing, and a thimble forecasts spinsterhood.

4. If you're a Polish child born on Christmas Day, you will become a werewolf.

5. Letting the fire in your fireplace go out on Christmas Day is bad luck.

6. It is bad luck to throw out your Christmas greenery (trees and wreaths). They should be burned in the fireplace instead. Judging by the number of trees thrown out on the curb, this is a superstition most American suburbanites don't believe.

7. Eat on apple at midnight on Christmas Eve for good luck.

8. In Scotland, the "First Footer"—that is, the first person who crosses the doorstep on New Year's Day—is very important. The ideal First Footer is a dark-haired young man, preferably carrying a lump of coal.

THE SIGNIFICANCE OF THE 3 GIFTS BROUGHT BY THE MAGI

The Book of Matthew specifically mentions that the Christ Child was presented with three gifts by the Magi: gold, frankinscense, and myrrh. To modern ears, those might sound like dull gifts. What exactly are those gifts, and how have religious scholars interpreted their significance?

A HOLIDAY POTPOURRI

1. GOLD (MELCHIOR'S GIFT)

    Obviously, we all know that gold is a precious metal. It is a symbol of Christ as king and reminds us that we owe God our virtue.

2. FRANKINCENSE (CASPAR'S GIFT)

    Frankincense was an expenseive form of incense in biblical times and thus stands for Christ as god. It reminds us that we owe god our prayers.

3. MYRRH (BALTHAZAAR'S GIFT)

    Myrrh was an ointment with medicinal qualties in biblical times. It is a symbol of Christ as healer and reminds us that we owe God our suffering.

6 POPULAR GARLANDS FOR YOUR CHRISTMAS TREE

1. Tinsel garland
2. Paper chains
3. Popcorn on a string
4. Dried cranberries on a string
5. Storebought beads and pearls
6. Ribbon

5 POPULAR TREE TOPPERS

1. Angel
2. Star
3. Santa Claus
4. Bow
5. Elves or pixies

7 NON-STORE BOUGHT ORNAMENTS TO HANG ON YOUR TREE

1. Cookies
2. Paper chains
3. Popcorn chains
4. Cranberry chains
5. Bread ornametns
6. Clove-studded fruits
7. Paper snowflakes

4 THINGS THE BIBLE *DOESN'T* TELL US ABOUT THE 3 WISE MEN

1. THEY WERE KINGS

   In the Bible, they are merely described as *magi*, which would indicate fortunetellers, magicians, and the like.

2. THERE WERE THREE OF THEM

   The Book of Matthew never mentions how many men followed the star (or, indeed, if they were men) but does mention the three gifts of gold, frankincense, and myrrh, which is why most people assume that there was one gift bringer for each gift.

3. THEIR NAMES WERE CASPAR, MELCHIOR, AND BALTHAZAAR

   These names are not mentioned anywhere in the Bible. Latterday legend has also supplied us with the "information" that Caspar was the oldest and that Balthazaar was black.

4. THEY EACH RULED SEPARATE KINGDOMS

   Popular legend tells us that Balthazaar was the King of Ethiopia, Caspar the king of Tarsus, and Melchior the king of Arabia. Again, the Bible says nothing about this.

THE BARE FACTS: 5 SPECIFIC PIECES OF INFORMATION THE BOOKS OF MATTHEW AND LUKE TELL US ABOUT CHRIST'S BIRTH

Although the image of Mary riding on a donkey to Bethlehem, being surrounded by barnyard animals, and being visited by three stately kings is familiar, the fact of the matter is that only two of the four gospels—Matthew and Luke—discuss Christ's birth, and only a few details of the birth are mentioned.

1. Jesus was born in Bethlehem. (Matthew and Luke)

2. There was an unusually bright star in the sky. (Matthew)

3. The Christ Child was visited by three magi—though we don't know how soon after his birth. (Matthew)

4. Jesus was born in a manger. (Luke)

5. Shepherds in the fields heard the angels singing and proclaiming the birth of God. (Luke)

A HOLIDAY POTPOURRI

3 SAINTS ASSOCIATED WITH CHRISTMAS

1. ST. NICHOLAS

   The inspiration for our modern-day Santa Claus was actually a Turkish bishop living in the city of Myra around 300 A.D. He has always been considered the children's saint; in fact, in the nineteenth century, *St. Nicholas* was the name of a very popular magazine for children. The real St. Nicholas is also associated with gift giving and chimneys. According to the legend, there were three sisters living in Myra who could not marry because they lacked dowries. Knowing they would not accept outright charity, Nicholas climbed on their roof and threw coins down their chimney, which landed in some stockings they had hung to dry. Whether the sisters ever married is not known.

2. ST. FRANCIS

   One of the most well known of all saints, St. Francis has long been associated with his love of animals and nature. His contribution to Christmas is the manger scene, which is still the center of Christmas celebrations (as opposed to the tree) in many European countries such as Italy and France. In order to make the story of Christ's birth understandable to the people (much as the miracle plays did in England), St. Francis constructed a nativity scene in a mountainside cave near the Italian village of Greccio. But this was no ordinary nativity, for the figures of Mary, Joseph, and the Christ Child were carved of wood and were lifesize. St. Francis also brought oxen and ass to the cave to re-emphasize the humble circumstances of Christ's birth. Although St. Francis did not invent the nativity scene, he is in large part responsible for its worldwide popularity, especially when we use it to teach children the story of the nativity.

3. ST. WENCESLAS

   Better known as good King Wenceslas (from the carol of the same name), he was actually a Bohemian monarch living around 900 A.D. He fought for Christian principals at a time when his country was not totally converted and eventually died at the hand of pagans at the tender age of 22. Today, there is a famous statue of him in Prague, Czechoslovakia.

6 BRAND NAMES WE ASSOCIATE WITH CHRISTMAS

1. COCA-COLA

    The soft drink has strong Christmas connotations because of the famous paintings by Haddon Sundblom of Santa Claus drinking Coke. Sundblom's artwork contributed to our collective image of Santa as a red-cheeked, larger-than-life figure.

2. LIONEL TRAINS

    The classic boy's toy for Christmas—usually circling the Christmas tree, weaving in and out of piles of gifts—may just be more of a gift for fathers than for their sons.

3. KODAK

    In order to preserve those Christmas memories, we need to have snapshots, and Kodak always rolls out the sentimental commericials at Christmastime to remind us that no film is as all-American as Kodak.

4. NORELCO

    Back in the 1960s, you couldn't get through a television Christmas special without seeing Norelco's whimsical animated commericials featuring Santa Claus using a Norelco electric shaver as a sled.

5. ANDRE CHAMPAGNE

   Another classic ad campaign from the 1960s, this one featured an instrumental version of "The Carol of the Bells" and many warmly lit photos of sophisticated adults clinking glasses of champagne and partaking in holiday cheer.

6. BUDWEISER

   During the holidays, Budweiser puts aside its football-and-partying image and replaces it with wonderful commercials featuring a sleigh pulled by Clydesdales gliding through charming villages and snow-covered countryside at twilight.

OTHER TITLES FROM KINGSLEY PRESS

The Christmas Book of Lists   ISBN 0-9637195-0-5 $7.95
Great Lovers and Couples   ISBN 0-9637195-3-X $12.95
The 10 Greatest Christmas Movies
　　Ever Made   ISBN 0-9637195-1-3 $7.95
Who Shares Your Birthday?   ISBN 0-9637195-2-1 $12.95

To order, write to Kingsley Press, PO Box 606-A, Downers Grove, IL 60516. Add $3.50 postage and handling no matter how many books you order.